ROCK HARP.

By Tony Glover.

Oak Publications
NewYork/London/Sydney

Illustration on page 76 by Eve Yost

Edited by Peter Pickow
Book design by Mark Stein
Cover design by Pearce Marchbank

International Standard Book Number: 0.8256.0230.0
Library of Congress Catalog Card Number: 80-84700

Exclusive Distributors:
Music Sales Corporation
225 Park Avenue South, New York, NY 10003 USA
Music Sales Limited
8/9 Frith Street, London W1V 5TZ England
Music Sales Pty. Limited
120 Rothschild Street, Rosebery, Sydney, NSW 2018, Australia

Printed in the United States of America by
Vicks Lithograph and Printing Corporation

Contents

Bob Dylan *photo by David Gahr*

Out Front

The harmonica has been used in recorded music for over fifty years now. In country music the "harp" could chord along with the fiddles, guitars, and banjos, and in blues it became the "Mississippi saxophone," its voice echoing the blues singer's cries.

In the bastard child of CW and blues; rock—the mouth harp is often used to add an especially funky feeling. It ranges from being heard occasionally as a backup sound, to being heard as a full fledged lead instrument.

Why the long lasting popularity of harps? Probably two main reasons; they're easy to play (you don't necessarily have to be able to read music) and they're relatively inexpensive, although the prices of harps have doubled over the last twenty years.

Harp has a very expressive sound—it's the closest yet of any instrument to the human voice. I started playing it because I wanted to sing, couldn't, but wanted to make music somehow. Harp is a useful lead instrument and when used with amplifiers, is equal in volume and intensity to any horn. A rock and roll player who can double on harp can bring another color of sound to the band he works with.

But you already know all this, right?

So, let's get down to some specifics. This book can teach a beginning player basic techniques, some theory and through exercises and examples from recordings you've probably heard, you can pick up the basics of several different styles of harp playing. The examples are written in a special form invented for people like me who don't read music.

In other words, this book is a place to start from, where you go with it depends on how much time and effort you're willing to put into it.

It differs from my two previous harp books, *Blues Harp* and *Blues Harp Songbook* in that the examples here are from the rock world. Much of the basic exercise work and theory is the same. You have to start with the same foundation—however, the approach is a bit different.

A word of caution; I said harp was relatively easy to learn and that's true, but it won't happen overnight. It takes practice, patience and a desire to get it right. Like most everything else, what you get depends on what you give.

Since you're still here, I guess you're into it. Let's get down, oh yeah. . . .

Picking a Harp— Buying Guide

There are several companies which manufacture harmonicas, but the one company with the widest line of models and the easiest availability is the M. Hohner company. Their general selection ranges from the *Little Lady* model (four holes, one octave) listing for $2.50, to a sixteen-hole chromatic with a four octave range (the *64 Chromonica*) running about $75. They also make various chord, bass, and specially tuned models, but you don't have to think about them unless you wanna get real weird.

The standard and most widely used model is the # 1896 *Marine Band*. It's a ten-hole diatonically tuned harp, which means it's tuned to the major notes in a particular key, like an octave on the piano, using whatever sharps and flats are needed in that key. It has a three-octave range, and at the time of this printing lists for $7.75. This harp comes pre-tuned (all the sharps and flats built in) in the keys of A, B, B-flat, C, D-flat, D, E-flat, E, F, F-sharp, G and A-flat.

The *Bluesharp,* is another model which is basically the same as the Marine Band, except the reeds are set higher. This makes it easier to *bend* the sound to get wailing blue notes. It comes in all the keys listed above, and sells for $8.50.

Another model to consider for special use is the *Vest Pocket,* (it's a smaller version of the Marine Band, three inches long where the Marine is four inches). You can cover more holes at once easily and it's handy if you want to make a lot of big, fat chords. The Vest Pocket comes in keys of A, B-flat, C, D, E, F and G/and lists for $7.50.

There are several other Hohner models which have the same tonal range and which are slightly cheaper in price, but my experience has proved that with regular use they wear out faster.

If you want to get into chromatic harps, which have all the notes available (the white and black keys of the piano) you have to make the necessary sharps and flats for the key you want to play in by pushing or releasing the slide lever as you blow. The *Chromonica,* a ten-hole model which comes in keys of C or G for $32.50, is a good choice. If you wanna go berserk, you can get a sixteen-hole model with a four-octave range, the *64 Chromonica* for $75.

So which to buy? A chromatic looks like it might be a good deal, since you can play it in any key, but. . . . to do that you have to get into a lot of theory, scales, and octave exercises—besides it's not quite the sound you want for most rock playing anyway. Unless you're a Stevie Wonder freak, you'll probably wanna pass on chromatic harps, at least for now. I'm playing at present with an acoustic trio that does blues, country, ballads, and rock and I use a chromatic at the most, on two tunes per night.

My personal preference, and that of most gigging harpmen I know is the Marine Band or the *Special 20* model. It's the same as the Marine Band except that the body is hard plastic instead of wood. The Bluesharp, which was first introduced a few years ago, seemed like a good idea at the time—it's reeds didn't need "breaking in" like the Marine Band, so it was faster and easier to play right off. But, over a period of time, my experience has been that it also tended to wear out (tones going flat, response getting mushy) a lot faster. So you'd be best to choose one based on how much you're gonna be blowing. If you're a full time player then durability is gonna matter. If you just feature harp on a few tunes a gig, then Bluesharp models might be right for you.

As far as what keys to start with, it depends somewhat on the kind of music and the kind of instruments you'll be working with in the band. If you're into basic three- or four-chord guitar rock music, you'll be dealing a lot with harps in the keys of C, A, and D. If you're blowing with a horn band then you'll use harps in keys of E-flat and B fairly often.

If you're serious about blowing with other people, and want to be ready to play on most tunes, the basic set would be harps in the keys of A, B-flat, C, D, E, F, and G. If you find you need minor or other key harps for certain numbers, you can always add them later on.

Breaking in Harps

When you get a new harp the reeds will be a little stiff. So it's a good idea to loosen them up by playing softly at first, say a few minutes a day for a week. This gives the reeds a chance to break in, and they're not quite so likely to go out of tune as if you've just started wailing full blast. Play softly at first, then gradually a little harder until you've worked up to your normal volume and strength. Takes time, but it's worth it. Nothing is more of a drag than picking up a new harp, wailing two numbers and finding out you've wasted a couple of reeds—if nothing else, it gets expensive.

It also helps to wipe off the mouthpiece after you're done playing. It doesn't take long for a layer of crud to build up. This doesn't affect the sound too much, it's just kind of nauseating. It's also not a good idea to blow harp between bites of a peanut butter and jelly sandwich.

There's a bit of a controversy over soaking harps. Some players like to do it, it increases volume and makes bending notes, easier, but it also swells the wood, which may cut into your lips a bit. It also voids any guarantees by the manufacturer—and is definitely not a good idea in any chromatic harp—the moving parts will rust and get weird real soon.

Soaking can be useful sometimes if a reed sticks (you get no sound at all or you get a very thin, tiny sound out of one hole), sometimes not. Basically it's up to you, whatever works best, whatever you can afford.

Some people soak harps in a large glass of water, others prefer to run them under a faucet. Basically, get the reeds good and wet, slap excess water out by tapping the harp on the palm of your hand, then play through all the holes to clear them. One more point— soaking reeds tends to make the pitch change a bit (usually a little sharp)—so you don't wanna do it just before somebody tunes his guitar up to your harp, he might have to re-tune later as reeds dry out.

If you do find that you wanna soak harps regularly, then the Special 20 is right up your alley—its plastic base doesn't swell and warp.

Other than the above, the only real consideration left is a hygenic one. Do you let anybody else play your harps? I don't, for two reasons 1) I don't let anybody else use my toothbrush either, 2) Each player has his own style and breaks harps in to fit that style—I'd rather not have a harp messed up by somebody other than me. I guess it comes down to how socially outgoing you are—just don't ask to use my harps.

The Mechanics of Harps

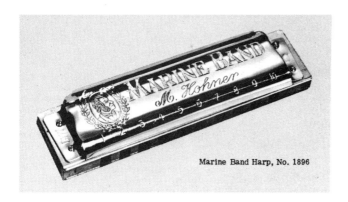

Marine Band Harp, No. 1896

Here is the Marine Band harp, which is the model used throughout the book, unless otherwise noted. If you have either a Bluesharp or a Special 20 model, no sweat, the tone layouts are the same, so everything that follows applies to them as well.

If for some destructive reason you were to take the top and bottom covering plates off, you'd see that the guts of the harp are two metal plates forming the top and bottom of a box, enclosed on the sides and back by wood (plastic on the Special 20), with ten holes on the front side.

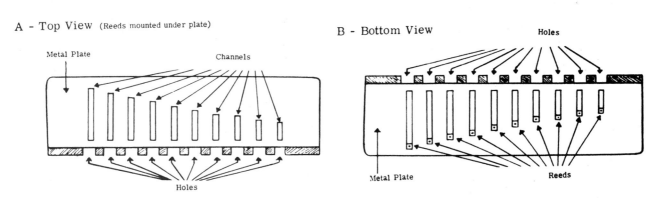

A - Top View (Reeds mounted under plate)

Metal Plate

Channels

Holes

B - Bottom View

Holes

Metal Plate

Reeds

Thin strips of metal, called reeds, are attached at one end, and placed so that they can vibrate freely in the channel cut for them. Dig that in the top view (A) the reeds are placed inside the box, and attached at the ends toward the mouthpiece (the side you blow into). In the bottom view (B), the reeds are mounted outside the box, attached on the side away from the mouthpiece.

The reason for this setup is so you can get two tones out of each hole, one by blowing, one by drawing. If you blow into the first hole, the one on the far left, the air will be forced to escape through one of the channels cut into the plate. Since you're blowing, it will go out through the topside (A, above), at the same time vibrating the reed in that channel, which produces a tone, with the pitch in direct relation to the length of the reed.

The longer the reed, the lower the tone, the shorter the reed, the higher the tone. Think about a piano for a minute. If you open it up, you'll see that the bass (low pitched) strings are much longer than the treble (high pitched) strings. This is also true on a guitar —when you fret a string up the neck you are actually shortening the part of the string which is free to vibrate when it is struck. The higher up the neck you go, the shorter the vibrating distance, and the pitch of the note will sound higher, dig it?

Okay, you're blowing into hole 1, the air escapes through the top channel, causing that reed to vibrate out and produce a sound. At the same time, the reed in the bottom channel of the same hole is pulled in, toward the inside of the box, but it doesn't vibrate, it just closes up the channel, so you hear only the tone of the top reed, a single note.

When you inhale (draw in) through hole 1 the opposite happens; the bottom reed (far left, B) will vibrate out as the air is pulled in over it, while the top reed is drawn closed, and doesn't vibrate. So again, you hear only the single tone of the one reed which is vibrating. In this way you can get twenty different tones from a ten-hole harp, two in each hole.

Now, check out the diagram below.

SCALE OF "C"

Notice this example is for a harp tuned in the scale of C. (Harps are manufactured in pre-tuned scales, with the reeds set to the necessary pitch for the key they're tuned in.) The *blow* notes are the large capital letters, the *draw* notes are the small capital letters. In the first hole, the blow note is C, the draw note is D, and so on up the scale. This harp (be it Marine Band, Bluesharp, or Special 20) is in what is called "diatonic tuning." This simply means that it's tuned the way you used to sing in music class; *do, re, me, fa, sol, la, ti,* and *do* again, one octave higher. In the key of C, C is *do* and the syllables which follow are all on the white keys of a piano.

Now, look again, and you'll see that there are some notes omitted in the first three holes —in fact the only complete eight tone scale is in holes 4 through 7. This particular setup makes playing chords possible, and the blues wailing sound as well. (More about this in a bit.)

If you have harps in the keys other than C (and you eventually will, if you're serious about playing) and you want to know the notes on them, you can use the above diagram as a guide. The tone relationships are the same no matter what key it is. The first blow note tells you the key the harp is in. For example, an A harp would be setup like this;

Hole 1, Blow—A   Draw-B
Hole 2, Blow— C♯   Draw-E
Hole 3, Blow—E   Draw-G♯

. . . .followed by a complete eight-tone octave starting with a blow note in hole 4. And so on. The relationships are the same, no matter what the key and the same notes are skipped or repeated in the same way. If you get worried about the sharps above, don't—the reeds are tuned to the sharps in the key of A.

If you have harps in keys other than C, try making a little diagram for each key following the tone layout above. It's good practice, plus someday you may need to find a G♯ tone—you'll know if you have it and where to find it.

Magic Dick *photo by David Gahr*

Beginning to Play

Let's assume you've never blown harp before. How do you hold it? The easiest way is whatever is most comfortable. If you're right handed, try holding it in your left hand, with the lower notes to the left, thumb below, and other fingers on top. Like this:

Your right hand is free to cup over your left and the harp and you can vibrate your right hand to produce tremolo (warbling) effects. If you're left handed, try the reverse. Hold the harp in your right hand with the low notes to the right. You can still cover the lower range of tones when you cup your hands this way. Once you've got that down, it's time to start blowing.

Let's kick off here with some simple, but necessary little exercises. First it's important to get a clear, strong, unblurry, single tone. Nothing is more of a drag than a sloplly mush-mouth harp sound. One method to use is "tongue blocking," shown below.

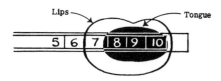

Your lips cover four holes, your tongue blocks off the three on the right, leaving only the hole on the left (7) open to sound. I find this a bit awkward so I use the "toke-taking" method. You just purse your lips as though you were taking the last hit on a roach or sipping from a tiny straw if you're a non-user. The point is that the opening between your lips should be no larger than the one hole on the harp you're trying to play. This may take a while, but it's worth the practice. To "bend" a note, you have to be able to get a single tone first, so you might as well start out the right way and not have to unlearn bad habits later.

Here are some exercises in a notation system developed by Thomas Hart Benton (Jackson Pollock was a pupil of his) and it works like this; the number tells you which hole to play, the direction of the arrow tells you whether to blow or draw. An arrow pointing *up* means blow out, an arrow pointing *down* means draw in while the length of the arrows indicate the length of time you should hold each tone. By the way, the notes above the numbers are for a C harp, if you're using one in a different key, ignore them and just go by the numbers, it'll sound just fine. Try this mother;

Hot Cross Buns

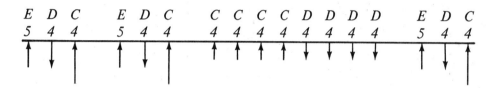

or the ever popular. . .

Mary Had a Little Lamb

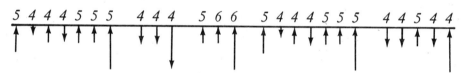

or get down with. . .

Row Row Row Your Boat

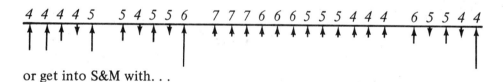

or get into S&M with. . .

Three Blind Mice

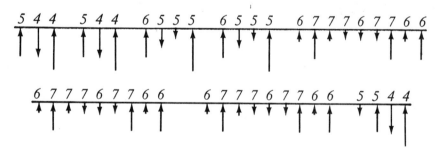

Work for clear single tones and easy transitions from one hole to another, try to get it to sound like a tune instead of just an exercise. Work on these until they flow and you're somewhat at home on the harp.

You may have noticed that the exercises above all use only four holes—4 through 7. This is because they are the only holes in which you'll find the complete eight-tone octave in the harp. Now if you check back to the diagram of tone layouts, you'll see that in the lower octave, in the first three holes, the A and F tones are missing. Later on we'll learn how to *bend* other notes to make those missing ones, don't worry about them for now. Here's one last exercise, might come in handy if you get drafted and have to go to summer camp.

Skip to My Lou

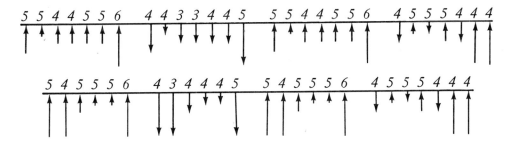

Another thing to think about, but not too hard, is breathing. You'll probably find that you're doing some around the harp, some through it, and some through your nose. Your body has a vested interest in itself, so it's gonna make sure that you get enough air in your lungs to survive, so just let it do what comes naturally. If you need to hold a note for a long time, then you'll have to take a bigger breath, if you got a lotta draw notes in a row and find your lungs getting too full, you can get rid of some through your nose while blowing out. Not smoking helps stamina too, but by and large breathing while playing should be as easy as falling off a ten-speed.

There are several ways in which harp can be used to accompany vocals, one is chording along behind the melody, the other is answering or echoing, in the spaces between vocal lines. A good example of this would be a tune like, "Please, Please Me" by The Beatles. You can find it on *The Early Beatles* (Capitol ST 2309). In this tune harp is used at the beginning as an introduction, and again between the vocal verses as a "fill," to echo portions of the song's melody line.

In this example, and others to come, something is added to the notation system. Each harp tone is represented by a phonetic word, which means that the word is approximately the sound of the harp note, mostly *wah, doo, ahh,* etc. Besides identifying the tone, this will help you get an idea of how to shape it.

Try talking through your harp once. Move your lips and tongue the way you would when speaking, but instead blow or draw through the harp for the sound. Try some *wah-wah* or *doo-doo* sounds. Experiment with some other sounds too, see what you can come up with. In the back of the book is a section which explains all the various different notation symbols and meanings, but for now we'll just add them as we go and they're needed.

The following phrase is similar to the one on the record. It's a simple seven-note phrase which comes twice at the beginning of the tune, and once after each verse;

Wah-Dee-Ahh   *Doo-Ah-Do-Ahh*   *A harp*
6↑ 5↓ 5↑   4↓ 5↑ 5↓ 6↑

Break this down and you'll notice that the phrase is in two just about equal parts—the first half is three notes, the second half is four notes, but both are played with in the same space of time as the three notes. The loop over the *Ah-Do* tones indicate that they're pushed together so these two notes are each one half the length of any of the other notes. Together they're equal to any one note in this phrase.

Blow out first through hole 6, shaping the sound *wah,* draw in through hold 5, shaping the sound *dee,* then blow out through hole 5 shaping the sound *ahh,* and so on. Remember, the looped together *Ah-Do* tones together take the same length of time as each of the other tones.

Try playing this along with the record to see how the timing works and how it sounds to your ear. If you have trouble hearing the harp, mess with the stereo balance knob to cut off one channel and you'll find the harp on one side in this recording, rather than mixed in the middle. Play around with this a bit.

Here's something to think about for a minute. If you were to play guitar along with this song, you'd find that it's done in the key of E. So naturally it would make sense to use an E harp, right? Well yes, but playing along with an A harp works just fine. Why? That's something we'll get into in the next section.

Cross Harp— Theory

You may find, at some point, that you don't have a harp in the key of the tune you'll be playing. *Cross harp* is transposing, or playing your harp in a different key from the one the tune is written in. Specifically, it is playing harp tuned a fourth higher than the harp which is called for.

A lot of the early classic rock songs, based on blues or country roots used a simple chord progression known as the I - IV - V progression. In twelve-bar blues, the most common type, the changes for one verse in a complete twelve-bar cycle would go like this;

Key of E

Bar 1	Bar 2	Bar 3	Bar 4	Bar 5	·Bar 6
E (I)-Tonic..................				(IV) subdominant	

Bar 7	Bar 8	Bar 9	Bar 10	Bar 11	Bar 12
E(I).......		B7(V)	A(IV)	E (I)...............	

In other words, to play a I-IV-V progression in E you would playing the following:

1. The I chord, E — bars 1 through 4.
2. The IV chord, A — bars 5 and 6.
3. I chord — bars 7 and 8.
4. V chord, B7 — bar 9
5. IV chord — bar 10
6. I chord — bars 11 and 12

This sequence would complete one verse in a twelve-bar blues cycle.

If this makes no sense at all, try following along with tunes like, "Down Home Girl" or "What A Shame" on *The Rolling Stones Now* (London PS 420). Both these tunes are in the classic twelve-bar pattern. Chuck Berry used variations on this basic progression for many of his early rockers as well. Listen for the chord changes in the guitar, see if you can count along.

Okay, let's say you're gonna be blowing harp along with a rock tune using this kind of a I-IV-V structure, say in the key of E. At the very simplest you'd be doing this;

Ist Position	E harp played in E	
Bars 1-4	blow hole 4	E
Bars 5&6	draw hole 5	A
Bars 7&8	blow hole 4	E
Bar 9	blow hole 3	B
Bar 10	draw hole 5	A
Bars 11&12	blow hole 4	E

Now let's try using an A harp with the same I-IV-V progression. Remember, we're still playing in the key of E, but this time we're using a harp tuned to the key of A. Like this;

Cross Harp	A harp played in E	
Bars 1-4	draw hole 2	E
Bars 5&6	blow hole 4	A
Bars 7&8	draw hole 2	E
Bar 9	draw hole 4	B
Bar 10	blow hole 4	A
Bars 11&12	draw hole 2	E

Go back to the chart for first position harp in E. You'll see that you're still playing the same pitches in each bar, however, you're playing different holes on a harp which is tuned to a different key. This gives us two of the three chords in our progression as draw tones and gives us some chord possibilities.

Notice that you're blowing two of the three chords in the progression and drawing on only one chord. So what? So this; By drawing you can get the distinctive wailing sound on harp you need in order to *bend* the pitch of the note, to slur it and make it cry the way guitar players bend strings to get notes to soar or drop. It's much easier to bend notes you draw than the ones you blow, I'm not really sure why, but take my word for it, I know it's true.

Once again, cross harp uses a harp tuned four steps higher than the key the song is in, while the harp is played in that higher key. (There's a reference table a little farther on.)

If all this sounds complicated and too much to mess with, dig that you've already done it. "Please, Please Me" was played in cross harp style. You were blowing an A harp in the key of E.

Here's another cross harp example, also from The Beatles, on *Meet The Beatles* (Capitol St 2047).

Little Child

A harp, cross position played in E

Intro

Wahh   Ahh   Dooo
23&4↓ 23&4↑ 4&5↓

1st Line

"Little child"   Wah-Wah-Doo
            3↓   4↑   4↓

2nd Line

"Little child"   Wah-Wah-Doo
            3↓   4↑   4↓

3rd Line

"Little child won't you dance with meee"
        Wah   *Wah*   *Wah*   *Ooooo*
        34&5↓   34&5↓   34&5↑   34&5↓

4th Line

"I'm so sad and lonely—Baby take a chance with me"
        Wah   *Wah*   *Ooo*   *Wee*
        4↓   4↑   3↓   4↑

whole section repeats

This covers the first verse of the tune, the rest is basically a repeat of the above with different lyrics, so once you've got this, you've pretty much got the tune covered. The first note in the introduction is a three-hole chord. You draw in on holes 2, 3, and 4 while shaping the sound *wahh.* Blow the same holes for the second note while shaping the sound *ahh.* The last note is a two-hole chord, drawing in on holes 4 and 5 while shaping the sound *dooo.*

The vocal line is sung in the first and second lines while the harp answers the line, with three notes echoing the melody. In the third line the harp comes in on the word "won't" with a three-hole chord (3, 4, and 5) shaping the sound *wah,* then again between the words "you" and "dance," and once more on the words "with" and "me." The fourth line has some single note sounds which come in while the vocal is being sung, just like the third line. If this looks strange to you, read it while listening to the tune, it should become clear.

Try playing along with this. Once again, play with the balance knob so you can cut out the vocals and concentrate on just the harp. Try to get a feel for the timing as close as you can by playing along.

If you're feeling adventurous, try playing along with the harp break, it uses many of the same patterns outlined above. By the way, the break was recorded as an overdub later, so it's on the stereo channel *opposite* the one that the harp's on.

Steve Forbert *photo by James Shive*

Cross Harp—
Chord Work
and Effects

Okay, the next step is to become familiar with this new position on the harp. It helps if you know where to find the I-IV-V chords as a matter of habit. These are fairly common chord changes found in many rock tunes. Other chords may be added or substituted, but they spring from that base.

Remember all the single note exercises, those lame little melodies? Well, they were all in *first position*—that is, you were playing the harp in the key it was tuned to. Here's a diagram which shows the difference between positions. Remember, tonic = I chord, subdominant = IV chord, and dominant = V chord.

Straight Harp (first position)

tonic	subdominant	dominant
4↑	5↓	3↑

Crossed Harp (second position)

tonic	subdominant	dominant
2↓	4↑	4↓

As always, arrows pointing up mean blow out, down mean draw in. If using names for those chords is a drag, you could call them by number. For example, in the key of E, E=I, A=IV, and B7=V. (As you count up the scale, A is the 4th note above E, B is the fifth, etc. Simple, right?)

At this point it would be really helpful to sit down with a guitar player and just mess with some changes in the I-IV-V pattern. Try playing along in cross position, get used to hearing the changes and making them without having to hunt around. Here's a table that'll help you tune with each other.

Second or Crossed Position

Use a harp tuned five steps (on the chromatic scale) above the key that the guitar is playing. Or, use a harp of the same tuning as the subdominant chord for the guitar key.

Guitar	Harp
E	A
A	D
G	C
D	G
C	F
F	B-flat
B	E

If you don't know any guitar players, try working along with records. Work on finding the right hole at the right time by feel, rather than by sight. Hit your notes as cleanly as possible, clear single tones without unintentional waverings. Later you may want to add colorful effects to your sound, but it's easier to add them than to try to take them out. In the words of the Vibrators, "Keep it clean."

The only way you're gonna get your sound together is by playing, there ain't any short-cuts. Play whenever you get a chance; whether it be fifteen minutes, four times a day, or an hour all at once, whatever works out best for you. The main thing is to listen to yourself, hear what you're doing both right and wrong. Then concentrate on polishing up what's right and fixing up what's wrong. Don't get discouraged if it doesn't happen the first, second, or even fourth time you try something new. Like anything worth doing well, it may take awhile. Learning how to play isn't a race with time or an endurance test. What counts is getting your chops clean and under control.

End of lecture, now on to something completely different. When you listened to "Little Child" you heard a warbling sound from the harp which shows up here and there throughout the tune. Here's how to do it.

Hold the harp as you would normally, let's say in your left hand, with the low notes to the left. Now take your right hand and lay the heel of it along your left thumb so that your right hand can close over the harp and over your left hand to make a cup. Now open that cup up, draw in on holes 2 and 3 together, and vibrate your right hand back and forth from open to closed. Dig that tremolo sound? See how you can vary it by changing the speed with which your hand vibrates. For an even wider tremolo, try pivoting your arm from the elbow and move your whole hand back and forth, from open to closed. Try playing around with this a bit; alternate between blowing and drawing on holes 2 and 3 together (always start and end with draw notes, this is cross harp position, right?) and you'll get a little train sound effect going.

Here's a good exercise for clean chops that'll be useful if you want to play *fill* rhythm type harp, like during the verses of a song, or while the guitar or horn players are soloing. What we're aiming for is the ability to cut off chords sharply. A chick I knew called it, "making it quack." Try it on the draw chord in holes 2 and 3. Play a chord, draw in as usual, then draw your breath in sharply, almost like a gasp, but even harder (a Jamaican toke), and at the same time pull your tongue back and away from the harp, toward the roof of your mouth, near the gums. If it doesn't work and you get a wheezy sound instead of a sharp ring, try the moves without the harp. Start where your tongue normally hangs out in your mouth. Now open your mouth a bit and suck in a chunk of air. Bring your tongue up to your gums as if it were trying to scoop the air in, hitting the gums hard enough so that you get a little *hut* sound. Now try it again with the harp.

Better? You may not be able to *kill* the sound sharply at first, but with practice it'll come. Now try cutting off the blow chord. Your tongue does just about the same thing. It should come fairly naturally and your breath should explode out, as if you were shooting a poison dart through a blowgun. Remember the phonetic words like *wah* and *doo* in the song examples? The idea again, is to talk through the harp letting your lips and tongue shape and form the words. Leaving your voice out of it, let the harp make the sounds. Let's use that same idea here. For each cut off chord, shape the sound *dit.* Draw in on holes 2 and 3, then cut off the sound, using the word *dit.* Try it in pairs (*dit-dit,*) cutting off the sound after each *dit.* For the blow chord, use the sound *dah* and try it in pairs, (*dah-dah,*) again cutting off the sound after each chord.

From that basic beginning, let's build a little train rhythm exercise. Although you may not be interested in Amtrak at the moment, this kind of chord work will be helpful later on in building rhythmic patterns.

To keep things clear in this exercise, we're gonna have to add the concept of time to our notation, in other words how long you hold a note in relation to the other notes. Instead of using arrows of different lengths, (that would be kind of complicated) to measure time we'll use a bar over the phonetic word sound, like this:

‾‾‾‾ ‾‾ ‾‾‾
dit-dit dah dah.
(In standard rhythmic notation: ♫ ♩ 𝅗𝅥)

Okay, what counts here is the number of lines, not the length of them. In the example above, the single line represents one unit of time. It can be any length you choose, depending on how fast you want to play. In this example, the *dah* tone has a single line over it, that's our reference point. The two *dit* tones are under a single line, which means that both these notes together are equal in time to that single *dah.* Or to turn it around, each *dit* equals one half the time of the *dah.* The final *dah* note has two lines over it. This means it should be held twice as long as the reference *dah* tone with the single line over it. If you were tapping your foot with this, you could tap once for both *dit* tones, once for the *dah,* and twice while holding the final *dah.* What counts more is how the times relate to each other, the length of each unit isn't too important right now. Okay?

Here's the start of our train rhythm type pattern; (Use holes nos. 2 and 3)

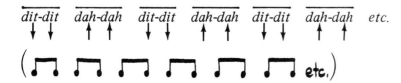

The time here is pretty simple; a *dit-dit* chord is equal in time to a *dah-dah* chord. Tapping your foot might help to keep the rhythm together. You can try tapping once on every single time unit, but later you might want to skip to every other or every fourth unit—when you get going faster, you'll probably have to, unless you're a tap dancer on the side. Try it slowly at first, then gradually build up speed. Concentrate on making the sounds equal in length and volume. Mess with it until you get it going fast and clean, without having to be consciously aware of blowing and drawing. It should come fairly easily after a-while.

As long as we've got a train hear (yes, that's a pun), let's toss in a whistle effect. After you've ended the phrase on a blow chord, try the following:

1. Move on up the harp to holes 3 and 4, draw in, and while cupping your hands, try the vibrating tremolo effect.
2. Blow out through the same holes using the vibrating hand tremolo.
3. Draw in, blow out once more, and return to your "chugging" rhythm chords.

These whistle chords should last about three or four times as long as the rhythm chords. You should be able to feel this, so they'll be written without time units, remember to hold them longer.

(Holes nos. 3 & 4 with tremolo)

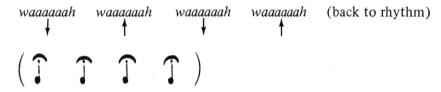

waaaaaah waaaaaah waaaaaah waaaaaah (back to rhythm)

Try working this whistle effect into the rhythmic pattern until it all fits together smoothly and strangers with luggage begin to appear.

Now let's get a little fancier, by changing the rhythm with the addition of another tone. Instead of playing *dit-dit* on the draw chord, say *da-DIT-dit*. The reason the first "DIT" is capitalized is to show that it should be hit a little harder and emphasized a little more than the other tones. Now let's substitute this phrase for the original draw chord and use the same blow chords, like this:

(Holes nos. 2 & 3)

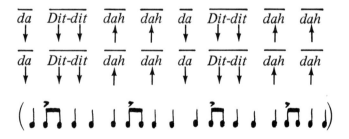

da   Dit-dit   dah   dah   da   Dit-dit   dah   dah

da   Dit-dit   dah   dah   da   Dit-dit   dah   dah

Dig how that changes the rhythm? What's happening here is that the rhythm is becoming a bit syncopated. What has actually happened is that we've taken the original *dit-dit dah-dah* phrase and made two notes out of the second *dit*. The new phrase takes the same a-mount of time to play as the first one, the added note gives it a little kick. Start slowly, get the emphasis right, get the *swing* feel clean and then when you've got all that covered, build it back up to speed. Right now control and timing is more important than speed, that'll come later with practice.

Now that you've got that down, let's spice it up a bit more. Our new pattern starts the same way, but for the blow phrase *dah-dah* let's substitute the sounds *hah-a-hah.* You blow out on the first *hah,* draw in on the *a,* and out again on the second *hah.* This sounds more complicated than it is but it's just fast in and out breathing. This *hah-a-hah* phrase takes the same amount of time as the original *dah-dah* phrase. Once again, a note has just been split into two notes, the first *dah* is now two notes.

Before you give up, try playing, that's easier than thinking about it.

(Holes nos. 2 & 3)

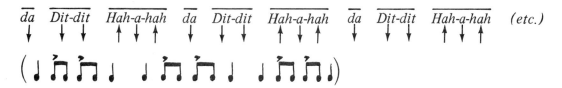

Remember, capitalized phonetics should be hit a bit harder for emphasis. Play with this until you've got the timing down and can get through it easily.

One of the tricks of learning harp is to make the playing process automatic as soon as you can, the sooner the better. You don't have to think about how to ride a bike or drive a car once you got the mechanics of the trip down—it's the same thing here.

Now let's mix it up even more. We'll alternate this phrase with the previous one, like this:

(Holes nos. 2 & 3 again)

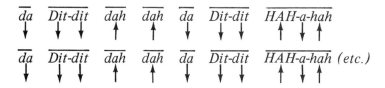

It might help to tap your foot in order to keep the rhythm steady. Try tapping once on the *da-DIT-dit* phrase and once on *dah dah* or alternate with the *HAH-a-hah* phrase. If this confuses you, try tapping more often, but tapping more will obscure the main beats.

Start slow and clean again, and speed up only when you can control it, don't get out of hand or mouth. This is a handy phrase to have, it works for a lot of rhythm accompaniment styles and you just vary it a bit to fit the different rhythms. This can be done by adding a beat, dropping one, or changing the emphasized tones.

Dig this. . .when you've played the above in holes 2 and 3, you've been blowing the I or tonic chord for cross harp style. If you move up the harp and use holes 4 and 5 it's the IV or subdominant chord. So, if we added a run to cover the V chord, we'd have a complete little pattern in the I-IV-V progression.

Try this:

1. Draw in on hole 1, same as hole 4, except an octave lower, and say *dah dit-dit-dit dah*.
2. Repeat this again, then blow out hole 2 — hold it awhile.
3. Blow out hole 3 — hold that awhile.
4. Do it twice again, draw in on holes 2 and 3 and add the tremolo sound with your hand.
   Totally confused? Here's a diagram.

(Hole no. 1)

$\overline{dah}$	$\overline{Dit\text{-}dit}$	$\overline{dit}$	$\overline{dah}$	$\overline{dah}$	$\overline{Dit\text{-}dit}$	$\overline{dit}$	$\overline{dah}$
↓	↓ ↓	↓	↓	↓	↓ ↓	↓	↓

$\overline{dah}$	$\overline{Dit\text{-}dit}$	$\overline{dit}$	$\overline{dah}$	$\overline{dah}$	$\overline{Dit\text{-}dit}$	$\overline{dit}$	$\overline{dah}$
↑	↑ ↑	↑	↑	↑	↑ ↑	↑	↑

(Hole no.2)

$\overline{\overline{doooo}}$ $\overline{\overline{dooooo}}$ $\overline{\overline{doooo}}$ $\overline{\overline{dooooo}}$
(2)↑   (3)↑   (2)↑   (3)↑

$\overline{\overline{doooo}}$ $\overline{\overline{dooooo}}$ $\overline{\overline{wahhhhhhhh}}$ *(hand tremolo)*
(2)↑   (3)↑   (2&3)↓

Check the timing on the long notes. The *doooo* notes are all two units long (two foot taps) while the *waaaaaah* is four. Run over this little phrase until you've got it together.

Now, if we paste all these little bits and pieces together we'll come out with a I-IV-V pattern which comes out to be twelve bars in length, the length of a verse or instrumental break in your basic rock format.

(Holes nos.2 & 3 tonic)

$\overline{da}$	$\overline{Dit\text{-}dit}$	$\overline{dah}$	$\overline{dah}$	$\overline{da}$	$\overline{Dit\text{-}dit}$	$\overline{HAH\text{-}a\text{-}hah}$
↓	↓ ↓	↑	↑	↓	↓ ↓	↑ ↓ ↑

$\overline{da}$	$\overline{Dit\text{-}dit}$	$\overline{dah}$	$\overline{dah}$	$\overline{da}$	$\overline{Dit\text{-}dit}$	$\overline{HAH\text{-}a\text{-}hah}$
↓	↓ ↓	↑	↑	↓	↓ ↓	↑ ↓ ↑

$\overline{da}$	$\overline{Dit\text{-}dit}$	$\overline{dah}$	$\overline{dah}$	$\overline{da}$	$\overline{Dit\text{-}dit}$	$\overline{HAH\text{-}a\text{-}hah}$
↓	↓ ↓	↑	↑	↓	↓ ↓	↑ ↓ ↑

$\overline{da}$	$\overline{Dit\text{-}dit}$	$\overline{dah}$	$\overline{dah}$	$\overline{da}$	$\overline{Dit\text{-}dit}$	$\overline{HAH\text{-}a\text{-}hah}$
↓	↓ ↓	↑	↑	↓	↓ ↓	↑ ↓

(Holes nos.4 & 5 subdominant)

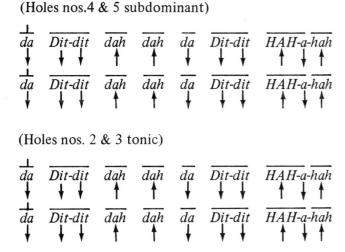

(Holes nos. 2 & 3 tonic)

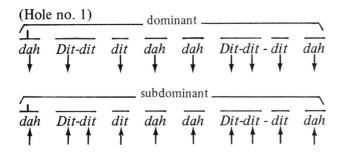

(Hole no. 1)

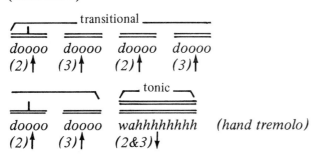

(Hole no. 2)

Try playing this all the way through until it makes sense, it's all stuff you've done before. This would be a good time to get in touch with that mythical guitar playing friend again, sit down with him, her, or it and con them into running some chords for you to play with. Try it fast, try it slow, should be fun.

By the way, notice this little vertical line on the time bars, at the beginning of each line? Each one of those counts as a bar. Add 'em up, and you get twelve. So, if you tapped your foot once on the *da dit-dit* and once on the *dah dah,* or alternated the *hah-a-hah* phrase, you were tapping four beats per bar which is a good, solid rhythm bass. Screw around with this until it becomes fairly easy, and so you can blow it without having to read and think about every note.

This is a good, basic rhythm pattern, but by no means the only one. Here's one way to change emphasis. In the example above you were coming in right "on the beat," at the same time as you tapped your foot. Try coming in on the up-beat, that is, when your foot is raised, and you're just about to tap. Here's a sample from one of the phrases before, only now the time is altered. Like this:

(Holes nos. 2 & 3)

da - Dit   dit   Dah   dah   da - Dit   dit   Dah   dah
↓   ↓   ↓   ↑   ↑   ↓   ↓   ↓   ↑   ↑

da - Dit   dit   Dah   dah   (etc.)
↓   ↓   ↓   ↑   ↑

It's the same phrase only the time is different. If you have trouble with the timing, try substituting these phonetics;
at-TACK the DOC-tor
Tap your feet on the accented, capitalized tones. See how the first *da* comes ahead of the tap. If you added the alternate *hah-a-hah* phrase and changed it to fit you'd get this:

(Holes nos. 2 & 3)

da - Dit   dit   HAH - a - hah   da - Dit   dit   HAH - a - hah
↓   ↓   ↓   ↑   ↑   ↑   ↓   ↓   ↓   ↑   ↓   ↑

da   Dit   dit   HAH - a - hah
↓   ↓   ↓   ↑   ↓   ↑

The rhythm here is equal to *at-TACK the DIR-ty dog.* See the possibilities? There are lots of ways to vary rhythmic accompaniments by making slight changes like this. Here again, playing with other people helps. You'll find ways to make things work and fit together better by doing it--and doing it--and doing it.

30

Rhythm Fills— Backup Work

Okay, it's a time warp, down the road a ways in time. You're playing harp with a band. What do you do when you're not taking a one or two verse solo? You could go play pinball, or hustle that number in the tight jeans over by the wall, but if you wanna stay on the stage and contribute to the music there are several things to keep in mind.

The first thing is, unless it's your band, your main job is probably gonna be to take occassional solos and the rest of the time to help fill out the sound. Many times you can work with the rhythm section and emphasize any rhythmic pattern they're laying down. Rhythm playing can be simple or complex. You can play one chord per beat or a lot more, but it depends on the tune and what fits. One of the main faults that most beginning, and some professional, harp-players fall into is just playing too damn much. You don't need to fill in every hole. Notes need space to breathe, and trying to play too fancy or too fast often ends up in calling attention to your technique and taking away from the total effect of the song.

Sometimes a rhythm similar to the last exercise fits in nicely during vocal verses or while other instruments are soloing, but the point to remember is that at that time someone else is out front either singing or soloing. Don't play too loud or too flashy, wait your turn, then come on like gangbusters.

On slower, ballad-like tunes, you might want to play long organ-like chords to make the overall sound richer. There again, just play off the changes, follow the progression. Listen to the rhythm guitar player and the lead player and try to fit yourself somewhere in between.

Your goal should be to complement the sound of the tune and to support the other musicians and singers, just like they'll be supporting you on your solo parts. Some musicians try to turn everything into "cutting contests" where everybody tries to play everybody else off the stage. That's okay once in a rare while, but in terms of making music that people are gonna want to listen to for more than seven minutes, cooperation goes a lot further than ego battles.

So part of your job is to fill out the sound. If there are no horns with the band, perhaps little *doo-wah* type horn fills between vocal lines or verses might fit. Perhaps a harmony part with the vocal melody line might be nice. . .lots of possibilities. The main point is that it all oughta blend together. If you stick out like a sore thumb during ensemble sections of the tune you're either playing too loud or the wrong riff.

You can have a good time even on numbers where you don't play any solos by finding a nice little riff which can complement whatever else is going down.

Once again, work off the changes, go with the progression, decide whether you want to play rhythm or melody fills (or maybe a combination), then concentrate on fitting it together. Just like the exercises, the way this works best is by doing. The only difference is, if you're playing in front of an audience you oughta have your trip together enough so that people can dig what you're doing, so be ready before you get on a stage.

Jam or rehearse whenever you can for the more you play, the more you'll know and the more you'll be able to do. If you aren't playing with people, then listen. When you go to hear a band, try to imagine what you would play with them, what kind of fills would sound good, what kind of rhythm or melody you would contribute.

Some Tonal Effects

There are a lot of ways to *color* the sound of the notes you get from a harp. Here are just a few, for openers.

First, draw in steadily on holes 2 and 3. Now move your tongue from where it usually is normally to the roof of your mouth. Try moving your tongue back and forth at different speeds. You'll get a little tremolo effect here which can also be used on blow chords.

A tremolo sound without using your hands comes in handy if you're planning on playing electric harp, where you'll be holding a microphone as well as the harp. First, without the harp, draw your breath in sharply, like a gasp, aim it toward the back of the roof of your mouth. Hear that little "cuk" sound? A dude I know tells me that it's the epiglottis clicking, the little trap door that fits over the pipes to your lungs. Its main gig is to keep food from falling into your lungs, and to let air in. What we're going for here is to use that mother about the same way you would in foreign languages where you need glottal stops, not to be confused with "pit stops." The back of your tongue lifts rapidly toward the back of your throat, closing the gap between your tongue and the opening of the throat. At the same time, something weird happens in your throat, but don't sweat it, unless you happen to be choking to death. Try to get a series of those stops close together, all in one intake of air. . .pretty much like a controlled spasm, or a deep sobbing. Now try it again, but this time draw in through a harp.

Get it? If nothing happens, try drawing in, and shaping the sounds *ca-ca-ca-ca-ca.* You don't want a series of separate stops or clicks. What you're aiming for is a flowing together tremolo sound that's smooth. This may be a bit difficult at first, but it's worth putting some energy into it. This will work on blow tones as well, but it's a little harder to control and to keep smooth. Work on this, but don't turn blue, that's bad form.

Another method for getting a tremolo is to use your jaw muscles. Open your mouth slightly, draw in through the ever popular holes 2 and 3. Now make your teeth chatter like they do when it's cold and you're freezing. You'll find you can get a very rapid tremolo this way. It works on both *in* and *out* breaths, although once again, the *in* breath is a lot easier to control.

One more tremolo method is one you may have already discovered, just screwing around. Draw in through the harp, hold your lips fairly firm, then take your free hand, the one that's not holding the harp, grab the harp and move it rapidly across your lips from side to side. Nice warble, huh? If you're planning on doing a lot of electric harp playing you might wanna learn to hold the harp still and get the warble sound by moving your head. This sorta depends on how heavy your microphone is.

In general the way you sound will be affected by the way you hold your mouth, the intensity with which you play (intensity is not the same as volume), and how you think. Harps are harps, they have a built in sound which doesn't change much from harp to harp, but you can color that sound alot by using warbles, tremolos, and cupping your hands. Harp players don't have to sound alike, only the lazy ones.

Bending Notes

There are a couple of reasons for *bending* or changing the pitch of harp notes. The first reason deals with the mechanics of how the harp tones are laid out, and the second deals with the theory of African-based blues tonality. Blues singers and players usually go along with the standard European diatonic scale—except in a couple of places. Two notes, the 3rd and the 7th of the scale are *blue* notes and they're generally pitched a bit flat. If you were to play a blues scale on the piano, the correct pitch for those notes can be found in the cracks between the 3rd and 4th keys and the 7th and 8th keys of the scale. These somewhat flattened tones give the blues its feeling of sadness and expressiveness.

The way in which the harp is laid out, there are two notes omitted in the lower octave, the 4th and 6th notes of the scale. Sometimes you'll need these tones and the way you'll get them is by playing the next highest note above the missing tone then flattening or bending it down to the pitch you need. You can make a note flat (lower in pitch) by bending a note, but you can't make it sharp (higher in pitch).

A physics student told me what happens when you bend a note. When you're playing harp in the usual fashion you are operating with a standard resonance system. A column of air vibrates in the harp and in your mouth cavity, which causes the reed to vibrate at its usual pitch, and produce its normal tone. When you bend or flat a note, you change the shape of your mouth, position of your tongue etc., which puts a different resonance system into operation and changes the pitch. I don't understand the fine points of it all, but I know it works.

To bend a note, you have to be able to produce a clear single tone just by narrowing your lips and leaving your tongue free. If you can't, then you've been rushing a bit. Go back to "Go" and don't collect $200. Begin by drawing in on the second hole, fairly hard. Notice how your tongue is in neutral, just laying around in the middle of your mouth. Picture how the air drawn in through the harp passes back in a straight line, over your tongue, to the back of your throat.

Okay, sing down the scale, one note at a time, and lower each time, till you're as deep as you can go. Notice how your lower jaw drops and tenses and how the whole front of your tongue drops to the bottom of your mouth cavity. Now sing your lowest possible note and bring your tongue back up to its neutral position. The pitch is raised some, isn't it? The point here is that dropping your tongue helps to drop the pitch a bit.

Basically, this is what goes on when you bend a note, you try to force or bend that column of air you're drawing in through the harp, down. Draw in on hole 2. Tense your lower jaw a bit and drop it some, bring your tongue down the bottom and front of your mouth and at the same time try to suck that air column down toward the tip of your tongue. Narrowing the size of your lip opening a bit also helps (bite down, pucker up!). It will take a fair amount of wind to do this and you need about twice the air pressure to produce a bent note of the same volume as a standard pitch note. The tip of your tongue should also curl back and down, sort of in an arch.

Any luck? If nothing happens the first time, don't get discouraged. Try again—and again— and again. It may drive you ratwire, but once you get it down, you'll wonder why you ever thought it was a hassle. Some people do it right off, others take awhile. The main thing is not to give up. If you ain't getting anywhere after a reasonable amount of work (you decide what's reasonable, I've got enough problems), then go back and work on some rhythmic patterns or tonal effects for awhile, come back fresh and try it again. It took me some time to get this covered, but it's worth the frustration.

If you've been using the tongue blocking method to get single notes, you might try bending by letting the edge of your tongue slip over and partially cover the hole you're playing, drawing in harder at the same time. The bend takes place with a very small movement of the tongue. It takes a fair amount of control and practice not to kill the tone altogether and practicing this kind of bending is really useful if you've got eyes to play chromatic harp. Chromatics have longer and stiffer reeds which are fairly difficult to bend with the lip method.

Whichever method you decide to use, the lip method is the most flexible, work to get a clear and unwavering tone. In other words it should stay bent on one pitch and should not waver back and forth. Here's a little exercise you can do with bent notes while you're waiting for a bus (or your Fiat). Go through the first four holes in sequence, starting in first position, like this:

1↑ 1↓ 2↑ 2↓ 3↓ 4↑

It's pretty obvious where the notes are missing in the scale, right? Now go through that scale again except now fill in the missing notes by bending the next higher pitched reed down to the pitch of the missing note, like this:

1↑ 1↓ 2↑ 2↙2↓ 3↙3↓ 4↑
          B   B

The bent notes are in holes 2 and 3 (shown by the bent arrows in the diagram). If you have a problem hearing the missing notes, try to find somebody to play the scale in the key your harp is tuned to on a guitar, piano or whatever. (If you can't find anybody who blows whatever, check places where dudes who double on etcs. hang out.) Don't be real fussy about getting the exact pitch at first, that'll come in time. The goal here is to make a completely natural sounding octave scale as fluid as you can.

Once you've got it down to a reasonable facsimile of a scale, try this: draw in on hole 2, bending the reed down to reach the missing note, D on an A harp, F on a C harp etc., this is the fourth degree of the scale. Now play the fifth note of the scale. This is a straight, non-bent, draw note in the same hole, but instead of making a sharp jump from bent to straight, try sliding up to it slowly. What should happen is your tongue should slide slowly up from the bottom of your mouth toward the harp, raising the pitch as it comes. Try this a few times and you'll notice that the closer in pitch the reed gets to the tone it was designed to make, the louder it will become so you must gradually decrease your air pressure as you're sliding to keep the volume the same.

Here's another sound that comes in handy. Slide up from a bent to straight note and when you're just about to reach the pitch of the straight note, open your lips up so you can get a chord in holes 2 and 3 (the I chord is cross-harp position) and at the same time, do a hand tremolo. Nice effect, huh?

Work on bending notes in other holes. The higher you go in pitch, the harder it gets to do. That's because the higher the pitch, the shorter the reeds are and the shorter they are, the harder they are to work with. It takes less tongue movement on the higher reeds to produce a bend than on the lower ones so control becomes more crucial. Generally speaking, you may as well forget about bending any draw notes above the 7th hole.

Notice I said *draw* notes, for on the higher reeds it's easier to bend blow notes. Bending a blow note requires a slightly different technique. Blow out through hole 7, with a lot of air pressure, purse your lips and narrow them down, and increase the air pressure even more. Instead of dropping your tongue down, tighten up a bit and move just a little toward your teeth. Any luck? This kind of bend will work on most of the higher reeds, but it probably won't on the lower ones. They are longer and take more wind than most people have to force them flat by blowing, so if you need to bend a blow note in the lower end of the harp, the tongue block method is probably best. It's the same way as before, the edge of your tongue covers the hole you're playing while you increase the air pressure. After you've messed with this a bit you'll see that draw notes are generally much easier to bend and control, but blow bends are possible, sometimes even necessary.

Another convenient point about the way tones are omitted in the harp layout is that they are missing in places where it's nice to use bent tones, like *blue notes* for transitions from one part of a chord progression to another like the I and IV chords, for example.

Say you've been playing a few rhythmic licks on the I chord, holes 2 and 3 of course, and you wanna go to the IV chord, here's a handy way to get there. Go up to hole 4, and draw and bend the tone down as far as you can. When you reach the limit of your bend, quickly switch to blow in the same hole, at the same time opening your lips so that you get a chord on holes 4 and 5. This should be a fluid phrase, a slur of notes run together instead of a separate sound. Starting with the I chord, it goes like this:

37

The first subdominant chord (IV chord) comes right after the transitional bend. Work on the transition alone a few times, then try it between the I and IV chord positions.

Let's add some chord fills on the IV chord and use another transitional phrase with bent notes to get us back to the I chord. It's a different one; draw in hole 3, bend it down as far as you can, then open your lips to a draw chord on holes 2 and 3. Like the previous transition, this should flow together, the notes shouldn't stand out by themselves. The difference between these two transitions is that we stay on a draw note here, open to a chord instead of going to a blow, then open to a chord. Here's the whole IV chord phrase with the transition back to the I;

```
         _____ subdominant _____
        /                                    \
  ___       ___       ___       ___
 dah-dah   dah-dah   dah-dah   dah-dah
  ↑4&5↑     ↑3&4↑     ↑4&5↑     ↑3&4↑

  _____              transition      tonic
 /                   \              ___   ___       ___
  ___       ___                    ═══   ═══       ═══
 dah-dah   dah-dah                dooo   oooo     dit-dit   (etc.)
  ↑4&5↑     ↑3&4↑                  3↓     3↲       ↓2&3↓
                                          B
```

This can all be played on an out breath, or several breaths, so it's gonna take big lungs or quick replenishing. Once again, the I chord comes in right after the transitional bend in a continuous smear of notes.

Since we've already got two of the three chords here, let's go all the way, hang out on the I chord until it's time for the V, but let's put in a little run instead of just chugging on a chord. Draw in hole 3, blow 4, draw 4, draw again on 4, but bend it this time and blow 3. The diagram looks like this;

```
  transition       dominant _____
 /          \      /                                          \
  ___   ___       ═══    ___        ___    ___       ═══
 dooo   ahh      doooo   dooo  -  oooo     ahh       (rest)
  3↓    4↑        4↓      4↓         ↲      4↑

 ( ♩    ♩    𝅗𝅥        ♩    ♩    𝅗𝅥      ▬    )
```

Pay attention to the timing here. *Rest* means just that—shut up for two time units. However this leaves us kind of up in the air, so let's add a resolving phrase with another transitional bend to get back to the I chord. Try playing it from the diagram;

(Holes nos. 2 & 3)

```
  ___     _____     ___     ___      ___    _____     ___    ___
  da    dit-dit    dah     dah       da    dit-dit   dah    dah
  ↓      ↓ ↓        ↓       ↑         ↑      ↓ ↓       ↑      ↑

  ═══     ═══      ═══     ═══
  da      dit      dit     dah
  2↓      1↓       1↓      1↓
```

Recognize the first part of this? Get that timing right, it's a handy little tag ending to use. Okay, if we put all these pieces together, we'll end up with a ten-bar chorus in a I-IV-V progression using bent transition notes. Ain't that hip? If it bothers you that it's ten instead of twelve bars, you can just add two more bars to the first I chord section and everything will come out fine.

Go through this until you've got it down pretty well. Get the bends working smoothly without wavers or wobbles. In other words, keep playing until it sounds like music. These kinds of transitions will come in real handy in any accompaniment you may be doing, especially on shuffle boogie type numbers.

Okay, you've put in a lot of work here on chops, here's a chance to apply them by playing along. Below is the harp break which follows the last vocal verse on the Rolling Stones version of "King Bee," *The Rolling Stones* (London LL 3375). Remember, bent arrows indicate a bend in pitch, bend the tone down. Time units are omitted here. You can hear it, right? Bear in mind that some of these phrases happen fast. So you won't have time to read it from the page. Think about it and then play along.

Try playing from the transcription until you're familiar with it, then put on the record and read the transcription with it. After it makes sense, try playing along.

If you've got a reel-to-reel tape machine you can stretch things out a bit. Tape the record at 7½ IPS, then play it back at 3¾ IPS—it will be an octave lower in pitch than the original, and the time will be doubled. The idea of course is to be able to play at regular speed. This taping trip is handy for working out parts you can't hear at full speed. Try playing along with this.

King Bee

(end break) A harp-cross position

(I)
Ahh–Ah-A–Whoooo   Do–Wahh–Ah–Doo
1↓ 2↓ 3↓ 2↓   2↘3↓   2↓ 1↓

            (IV)   (I)
Do–Wah–Ah–Wah   Do–Wahh–Ah–Dooo
2↘2↓ 3↓ 2↓   2↘3↓   2↓ 1↓

       (V)   (IV)   (I)
Ah–Ah–A–Wahh   Wee–Ah–A–Wah–Wah-Doo
3↓ 4↑ 4↘4↓   6↑ 5↓ 4↓ 3↓ 3↓ 2↓

A–Wah-Hah-Doo   Ooo–Wah–Doo
2↓ 4↑ 3↓ 2↓   2↘ 3↓ 2↓

A–Wah–Wah-Doo   A–Wah–Hah–Doo
2↓ 2↓ 2↘ 2↓   2↓ 4↑ 3↓ 2↓

A–Wah–Wah–Doo   Wah–Wah–Doo
2↘2↘ 3↓   2↓   2↘ 2↘ 2↓

                                       fades out

Basically you see, the harp is playing an echo of the vocal line. A few phrases are repeated, and some are similar with only slight variations.

In this break there are also a few *ghost notes.* They're there, but they happen so fast that it's hard to hear them clearly. If they weren't there, you'd probably notice their absence. The third tone in the first line is one of those, the draw on hole 3. It's just a flick of an eye in length, but it adds an important little lift to the piece. The dotted line marks the end of one chorus, although as you can hear on the record, the harp plays through the turn-around as if it were all on one line.

Play with this awhile, until you can get fairly close to sounding like the record.

At this point, it's a good idea to go back to the beginning of this whole section and do a little review number. Make sure your bends are under control, clean and strong and that you can do clean and sharp rhythm and cut-off chords. In general clean up any loose lips, and tighten up your chops.

It might also be a good idea to put this book aside for awhile, and see what you can do by yourself. Anything you discover on your own will stay in your mind faster and firmer than anything anyone can ever tell you. William Burroughs the writer says, "You can't tell anyone anything they don't already know."   He's right. Listen to records, look for bent notes and rhythm chords, figure out what's going on, and see if you can figure out how to do it. By now you oughta have a good handle on it.

If you're starting to brag on yourself, try this—I know a dude who can get four separate and distinct notes from hole 1 draw on a G harp. If you can do it, you got a right to signify. Until then, we're all just learning. . . .

Roots: Blues

Rock and roll came from two native American musical sources, C&W and blues. Chuck Berry's "Maybelline," was one of the first recordings by a black artist played on country radio stations. Elvis Presley's "That's All Right Mama," was one of the first recordings by a white man played on R&B radio stations. The reason was that these styles were merging into a new form, soon to be called rock and roll. Harp was used regularly in blues recordings and fairly often on country singles as well for it's got that vocal, expressive sound.

The Rolling Stones were the first of the popular rock groups to do fairly faithful renditions of older blues tunes. Over the years they have covered versions of songs by bluesmen like Muddy Waters, Jimmy Reed, Slim Harpo, and Howling Wolf, all of whom use harp on their recordings as a matter of course. So in many ways the roots of rock harp are in blues. In fact, until recently, most rock harp playing was white kids doing a very poor job of trying to play black music. John Lennon's early recordings of harp playing on Beatle albums is fairly simple by blues standards, he's wheezy in sound and limited in ability. But, a new rank of harp players is emerging. There are people who have studied and become fairly adept in roots styles and gone on to create their own unique, individual sound.

To build you gotta have foundations, so here's some blues foundation. Here's an early bluesman in the Chicago style, Jimmy Reed. He was born in Mississippi, but began recording after he moved to the Chicago area. His music is a mixture of down home soul and the rougher edged and amplified city sound. Several of his 45's were hits in the early days of R&R, and his harp style has influenced a lot of players. Most of his recordings were built around variations of a simple walking bass twelve-bar, guitar boogie style. The harp was used as a piercing high note punctuation and carried most of the instrumental breaks. He recorded for the Vee-Jay label from 1953-1965, and put out several albums on various labels before his death.

"Going to New York" is a typical up tempo Reed number. A cover version can be found on an album by the Climax Blues Band, but the original is on a double album, *History of Jimmy Reed* (Trip TLP 8012). Reed played both guitar and harp, with the harp in a holder worn around his neck, so all effects are done without the use of his hands. The tune is in the first position (A harp played in A). This is a transcription of the break. It's a full twelve-bar chorus, and follows the second vocal verse;

Going to New York

(break) A harp in A

(I chord)

Doo—Ah-Wahhhhhhhhhhhhhhhhh
8↑ 9↓ 9↑

Ah—A—Oooo
9↑ 8↑ 7↑

(IV)

Wah—Ah—Ah
8↑ 8↑ 7↑

Wah—Ah-Ooo
9↑ 8↑ 7↑

(I)

Wah-Oooooooooooooooo
8↑ 9↑

(V)

Wah—Ah—Ah
8↓ 8↑ 8↓

(IV)

Ooo—Wah—Ah—Doo—Wah
9↑ 10↑ 10↑ 8↑ 7↑

(I)

Looks pretty simple, right? Try playing along. This is good practice for single notes, and also gives you a workout in that higher octave, not a place you'd want to stay all the time, but it's nice to drop in now and then for effect. The same album set includes two other numbers which turn up frequently in the repertoire of blues-rock groups, "Big Boss Man" and "Bright Lights, Big City," the latter is also in A, first position. Basically, you can play along with almost any tune on this album. Find the key with the help of guitar, piano or your own ears, then dig all the changes, and try to make them. Even if you can't right away, it won't hurt to try, the experience will help.

Another important and influential blues harp player was Little Walter. He recorded with Muddy Waters on most of his early hits, then later formed his own band. Every bluesharp player who followed owes him a debt. He was the player who made the most use of electric (amplified) harp. Instead of being content with it being louder, he took advantage of effects like echo and tone controls, to make the harp a solo instrument and put out several instrumental 45's featuring harps which were R&B hits. Walter's style came out of the blues, but he was also jazz like in his concept and musical execution. Two current players who owe a lot to Walter are Paul Butterfield and Magic Dick of the J. Geils band. The following is an early effort with his own band. "Last Night" is on the double album *Little Walter* (Chess 2 ACMB-202) and is a good example of his soulful, funky, and creative style. The transcription here covers the instrumental break following the second verse;

Last Night

(break) G Harp, crossed

(I chord)

Ah-Wahhhhh
4↘ 3-4-5↓

Ah—Wahhhhh
4↘ 3-4-5↓

Ah-Wahhhhh
4↘ 3-4-5↓

Wah-Ah-Ah-Doo—Ah-Ah-Doo-Ah-Ah-Doo—Ah-A-Doo-A
3↓ 4↑ 4↓ 5↓ 6↓ 6↑ 5↓ 5↑ 4↑ 3↓ 3↑ 2↑ 3↑ 4↘

(IV)
Wahhhhhhhh
  3-4-5↑

Wah—Ah-A-Wahhhhh
4↓   4↑ 3↑3-4-5↑

(I)
Wah-Hah-Ah-Wahhhhh
3↓ 4↑ 4↲3-4-5↓

Ah-Wahhhhh
4↲3-4-5↓

(V)
Wah-Hah-Ah-A-Do-A-Ah
4↓ 4↑ 3↑ 3↓4↓ 3↓2↓

(IV)
Wah-Ah-Do-Ahh
3↓ 4↑ 3↓ 2↓

(I)
Ah-Ah-A-Wooo
2↓ 2↑ 1↓2↓

Wahhhh-Wahh—Ah-Doo
3-4-5↓ 3-4↓ 3-4↓2↓

(V)
Wahhh-Ah-Ah-Do
2↓   2↲1↓ 1↓

Wahhh
2↓

This is getting a bit more complicated, right? Read it through a few times, try playing it slowly, read it through while listening to the record, then try to put it all together. As you listen, you'll notice that the loop under *Wahhh-Ah* under the final V chord in the last line indicates that those notes should be slurred. First hit the note, then bend it without a break in between.

This is just the tip of the iceberg, there are many excellent bluesharp players worth checking out, like Sonny Boy Williamson (the second, the one who recorded for Chess label in Chicago) and Sonny Terry, who has more of a folk blues style. If you really want to get into it, check out *Bluesharp* and *Bluesharp Songbook*. They cover much of the same basics, but go into various aspects of blues style in more depth.

Even if blues ain't your bag, you oughta be aware of it and the importance blues had in contributing language sounds and riffs to the world of rock. Familiarity with where it came from won't hurt you none, it might even help you some.

Bruce Springsteen *photo by James Shive*

Roots: Country

Country music and the folk forms which it came from are another main influence on rock harp. Harp can be heard in old-timey string bands. Roy Orbison's early Sun label singles, and both Waylon Jennings and Willie Nelson feature harp on their recordings and in their performances. In the song arrangements of both these singers, harp is used mainly for fills, like in a response to a vocal line, and occasionally takes the lead during an instrumental chorus.

Willie Nelson employs Mickey Raphael as his full time harpman. Raphael worked with several folksingers before becoming a regular with Nelson in 1973. His playing ranges from country folk to funky soul. It is colored by a clear, sweet tone and the good sense to know when not to play. (There are times when the best thing a musician can do is to shut up for awhile.) The following is a sample from Nelson's *Red-Headed Stranger* album (Columbia KC 33482), the tune is called, "Can I Sleep in Your Arms Tonight Lady." The harp break is taken on the last chorus, following the last vocal verse. Here is the whole thing;

Can I Sleep in Your Arms Tonight Lady

A Harp, cross position

(I chord)
Ahhh-Ah-Oooo	*Ahh-Oooo*	*Ah-Woo-Ahhhhhhhhhh*
1↓ 2↑ 3↓	4↑ 4↓	3↓ 3⤸ 3↑

		(V)
Ahhh-Ah-Oooo	*Wah-Ah-Ooo-Wah*	*Ah-Eeeeeeeeeeeee*
1↓ 2↑ 3↓	3↑ 3⤸3↓ 4↓	5↑ 4↓

(I)		(IV)
Ah-Wa-Ah-Eee	*Ooo-WAHH-Ahh-Wah-Ahh-Ooo*	*Wah-Ahh-Ah-Wooo*
3↓ 4↓ 5↓ 6↑	6↓ 7↑ 6↓ 6↑ 5↑ 4↓	5↑ 4↓ 4↑ 3↑

Wa-Ha-A-Oo   *Ahh-Ooo*   *Wa-Ha-Ah-Ooo-Ah-Ah-Ooo*
2↑ 2↓ 3↙ 3↓   4↑ 4↓   5↓ 5↑ 4↓ 4↙ 4↑ 4↙ 4↓

Wah-Ahh-Ooooooooooooooo
3↓ 3↙ 3↑

Check out the phrase at the end of the fourth line in holes 4 and 5 under the V chord. It's a fairly common transitional fill and a nice way to get from one chord to another. Remember, the capitalized phonetic in the third line *WAHH* indicates that this tone should be hit and emphasized a little more than the other sounds. Dig the slight tremolo coloring used on the notes that are held awhile. This is worth working on, and getting it to sound as close to the record as possible. In fact any of Raphael's work would be worth studying if you plan to do any country-oriented blowing. He combines the melodic melancholy of country with the dirty edged funk of blues and rock plus he's a clean and tasteful player.

Another ultra-clean player is Charlie McCoy. Besides several of his own albums, he's been session man with musicians as diverse in style as Elvis to Bob Dylan, and from Perry Como to Simon and Garfunkel. His harp is the one you hear on most Nashville sessions. One of his solo albums features a version of "Orange Blossom Special" which has veteran harp blowers shaking their heads in awe at his speed and precision. His albums are on the Monument label, and are worth looking into.

Country harp, as with blues, is one of the foundation sounds for rock, so the more you listen, the more you'll have stored in your head to use when you need ideas. Besides, the more you listen to various kinds of music, the more flexible and inventive you'll be in playing your kind of music.

Electric Harp

No, it's not a harp you plug in and watch play by itself. Electric, amplified harp means playing the harp into a hand held mike which is connected to a separate amplifier. This method was first used by Chicago bluesmen like Little Walter and Sonny Boy Williamson for the simple reason that they wanted to be heard over drums and electric guitars.

More than just making it audible, amplification affects the tone of the harp and the instrument's role in the band. If harp is played through P.A. mikes, you'll find often that you'll be fighting for space with a vocalist, but with your own amp it's no problem. When you use your own amp, you have much more control over the tone and volume of your sound than if you're going through the P.A. Some players prefer to hand hold a mike and go through the P.A., rather than their own amp. The advantage is you don't need to haul around that extra amp. The problems are you can't hear yourself, unless you're using a P.A. which has good monitor speakers and you're subject to the needs of vocalists for mikes. Whether or not you'll want an amp depends on the situation. It depends on how much playing you do in the course of a gig, and how necessary the electric sound is.

What kind of mike? The old bluesplayers used to use whatever came in handy. They were usually fairly cheap, but durable models with rather poor fidelity, so they built in a kind of fuzz-distortion sound. When younger players tried to get that funky blues sound and had problems, they figured it might have something to do with the equipment, so they'd go out and get an old beat up mike, but the sound was still not right. The secret is that it's in the player as much as the equipment, although equipment does affect the sound. Many bluesplayers toured overseas and played concert halls rather than bars. They were exposed to better quality sound equipment and as a result they altered their sound a bit to get that funky edge, even through hi-fi sound systems.

There are a couple of mikes especially designed for use with harp. One is the *Hohner* HH9911 selling for $52.50. The mike is mounted in the middle of a hard shell case in which the harp fits. Personally, I find them useless—the tones in the middle are overemphasized, they're right near the mike, while notes on either side are too low in volume. They're probably good for lounge bands that do a lot of polkas. If that's not your bag, read on.

What kind of mike? I've seen almost everything used from little telephone kind of mikes, up to expensive recording studio models and it seems that generally, the low to medium-priced ranges have a better sound.

There are two main types of mikes used for P.A. work, crystal and dynamic. Those terms refer to the way they convert sound to electrical impulses. Dynamic mikes are usually tougher and more durable than crystal mikes which tend to work inefficiently after being dropped or knocked around a few times. Crystal mikes have a tendency to *blast out* (distort annoyingly) when blown into from close up. This is what you're doing when you hand hold a mike. You'll also want one that's fairly directional (picks up sound in one direction rather than from all around) to avoid feedback, that pain-in-the-ass squeal when a mike is too close to a loudspeaker.

If you're planning to plug the mike into an amp, then you'll want one with high impedance, a measure of resistance and other electrical characteristics. Many P.A. mikes which connect directly to a mixing board are low impedance, however, you can get transformers which will convert from high-to-low or from low-to-high. The majority of instrument amplifiers, however are all high impedance, so figure out which one you may have more use for, then buy accordingly.

Another thing you'll want is a heavy duty cord; no matter how cool you are, you're gonna get your cord walked on onstage, if not by you, then by a guitar player, or soundman or even rampaging fans. The wires inside the cord will be broken after stomping on it enough times and the heavier your cord, the less you'll have to worry about it shorting out.

About the easiest way to select a mike is to figure out your price range. It is realistic to plan on spending from $20-$60 for a new model. Try them out, play them through the amp you'll be using. Check for tone range and distortion free sound reproduction. Can you make it fuzz when you want or does it fuzz more than you want? Another thing to consider is weight. If you're gonna be holding it to your mouth and blowing all night, it's gonna get heavy, so you'll want something you're comfortable with. To sum it up, go with what you can afford and what feels best, as long as it gets the sound you want.

Okay, amplifiers. Here again, it depends on what you want and need. Are you gonna be blowing with a band that only has a vocal P.A. and uses the instrument amps to fill the room? Then you'll need a fairly powerful amp to hold your own. Or does the band mike all the amps and feed them through the P.A.? Then you can get away with much smaller models with less power.

For several years I used a *Fender Twin-Reverb* amp which has two twelve-inch speakers and all the power you need for most bands. It also has effects such as reverb (echo) and tremolo vibrato. Lately, I've been working with acoustic guitars and using a small, cheap, Sears two-tube model. It's got exactly the sound I need and it's loud enough in small clubs. In large ones, I just mike it and feed it through the P.A.

An amp that has *reverb* is nice. That echo sound makes it fuller and deeper. You'll have to be careful though about volume and position when playing amplified for if you stand right in front of your amp and turn it up, you're gonna get that feedback howl. Experiment, try various positions in relation to the amp, various tone settings (you won't want to use full treble for example), and different amounts of reverb. All of these things are interrelated and affect each other, it's a balancing process.

As far as cost, it depends on whether you're looking at new or old models, big or small sizes. Remember, it's not automatically true that new and high priced amps are better. I like the sound of that battered little Sears amp more than my brand new Fender. Again, let your ears be the judge. Get the power you need and the sound you want.

Electric harp is heard on more and more rock country and pop recordings and is played by people like Paul Butterfield, Lee Oskar, (formerly with War) many blues players, and on a few songs for special effect by Mick Jagger. The following is a transcription of the introduction and fills for the first verse of "Midnight Rambler" from the Stones album, *Let It Bleed* (London NPS-4). Jagger overdubbed the harp and so you'll hear him singing the same time the harp starts to play a response.

Midnight Rambler

(Words and Music by Mick Jagger and Keith Richard)

Introduction & 1st Verse   E harp, cross position

guitar riffs, then/

Ooo-Wahhhhhh	*Doo-Ahh-Ooo-Wah*
3↓ 3&4↓	2↓ 2↓ 2↵ 2↓

Ooo-Wahhhhhh	*Doo-Ahh-Wah-Ooo*
3↓ 3&4↓	2↓ 2↓ 2↵ 2↓

Ooo-Wa-Dooo-Dooo	*Dooo*
2↵ 2↓ 2&3↓ 2&3↓	2&3↓

Did ya hear about the midnight rambler
                    Ooo—Wah—Ooo
                    2↵ 2&3↓ 2&3↓

Everybody got to go
              Doo-Wah   *Wah—Doo—Ahh*
              2↵ 2↓   2&3↓ 2&3↓ 2&3↓

Did you hear about the midnight rambler
                    Ooo—Wah—A—Ooo
                    2↵ 2↓   2↓ 2↓

The one that shut the kitchen door
                    Ooo—Wah—Ooo—Ooo
                    2↵ 2↓   2&3↓ 2&3↓

Don't give no hoot 'bout a warning
                    Ooo—Wah—Ahh—Ooo—Ooo
                    2↵ 2↓   2&3↓2&3↓2&3↓

Wrapped up in a blackjack cloak
              Ooo-Wah   *Ah—Ooo-Ooo*
              2↵ 2↓   2&3↓2&3↓2&3↓

He don't go in the light of morning

            Ooo—Wah—Ah—Ooo-Ooo
             2⤵ 2↓   2↓ 2&3↓2&3↓

Worried that the cock'll crow

            Ooo—Wah—Ah—Ooo
            2⤵ 2↓   2↓ 2↓

Ah-A-Ooo-Ooo	*Ah-A-Ooo—Ooo*	*Ooo—Ooo*
L⤵ 1↓1&2↓1&2↓	L⤵1↓ 1&2↓ 1&2↓	2&3↓ 2&3↓

Ah-A-Ooo—Ooo	*Ah-A-Ooo—Ooo*	*Ah-A-Ooo*
L⤵1↓ 2&3↓ 2&3↓	L⤵1↓2&3↓ 2&3↓	L⤵1↓2&3↓

Talk about the midnight gambler. . .

The rest of the song follows this pattern fairly closely, so you oughta be able to get it from this sampling. Further into the piece warbles are used more (the type in which the harp is moved sideways and back and forth across the lips). Remember, the tone is affected by the amp, so if you're trying this acoustically you won't be able to get the exact tone color.

Electric harp playing is the same as acoustic harp in that the best way to learn is by doing. Sit in with bands whenever you can, play with records. Experiment with different amps and settings, get used to using your equipment and getting the most out of it. Just remember that what you put *into* it comes first.

Chromatic Harmonica

Chromatic harps are used only now and then in rock music. They're bulkier, harder to play and a lot more expensive. However, for certain sounds and styles, they work really well. Chord style playing on a chromatic is more difficult, however, due to the way the tones are laid out, but consequently melody playing is somewhat easier. If you know your scale, you can play in any key on one harp.

Remember way back there when we said that the Marine Band and the similar ten-hole harps were laid out in diatonic tuning? (An eight-tone scale, like the white keys in the key of C on the piano.) The drawing below is of a *Hohner Chromonica 260*. What it amounts to are two harmonicas, one placed on top of the other. By means of a push button slide lever, the top harp holes are left open while the bottom are closed off, or vice-versa. In the key of C, chromatics are generally tuned to start with either a C or G note, the bottom harp is tuned diatonically in the key of C♯, the top harp is tuned diatonically in the key of C.

This shows a full view of the Chromonica mouthpiece. Arrow points to the lever.

With the lever in its normal out position, (a spring keeps it there) you're playing through the C harp and when you push the lever in you're playing through the C♯ harp. You can get four different tones from each hole; one blow and one draw with the slide in and one blow and one draw with the slide out. This duplicates a piano, white and black keys.

Here's the tonal layout:

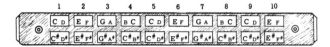

Again, the top row of notes are for the C harp (slide out), the bottom row of notes for the C♯ harp (slide held in). In both cases, large letters are blow, smaller letters draw.

If you have a chromatic harp (I wouldn't buy one unless you got bread to spare, and/or plan to be blowing it a lot) try playing a scale up the octave. Blow hole 1, with the slide as it normally is, out. Then push in on the slide, using your index finger, blow again and you will get a tone one half step higher in pitch. Release the slide and draw hole 1 a tone a half step higher again. Push the slide in and draw again—another half step higher tone.

And so it goes until you get to hole 4 where the draw note is lower, rather than higher. Why? I guess it's so all the C tones on the harp will be blow tones, no matter where you find them. You'll also notice some repeated tones; hole 2 blow/slide in is the same pitch as hole 2 draw/slide out and hole 4 draw/slide in is the same as hole 4 blow/slide out. How come there aren't any repeats on the tonal layout? That's because there really ain't tones like B♯ and E♯. See the drawing of a piano keyboard below:

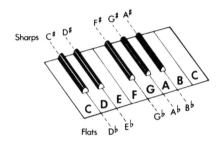

There aren't any black keys between B and C and C and F, right? So what the layout calls B♯ has the actual pitch of C, and E♯ has the same pitch as F. Why not call them by their right names? You got me—something to do with some advanced theorectical application, which doesn't have a lot to do with reality. (Then again, I don't have a lot to do with reality either, when I got a choice.)

Anyhow, the upshot of this mess is that you can play 2½ octaves, with all the same notes, white and black keys, that you'd find in 2½ octaves on a piano. So if you started in the right place, you could play a chromatic in any key.

Marine Band harps make it easy for you. They're pretuned with all the necessary sharps and flats built in, but with a chromatic harp it's up to you to do it. You have to know each scale's sharps and flats and stick 'em in at the right time. If you can read music you'll be ahead of the game for chromatic harp, it'll just be the mechanical work you'll need.

Here's a table of the seven major scales;

Key	Scale
A	A, B, C♯, D, E, F♯, G♯, A
B♭	B♭, C, D, E♭, F, G, A, B♭
C	C, D, E, F, G, A, B, C
D	D, E, F♯, G, A, B, C♯, D
E	E, F♯, G♯, A, B, C♯, D♯, E
F	F, G, A, B♭, C, D, E, F
G	G, A, B, C, D, E, F♯, G

To learn keys you have to know the scales. Start with the lowest note available in whichever key you're practicing. (A—hole 3 draw, B♭—hole 3 draw/slide in, etc). Work your way up the scale as far as you can go, putting in the appropriate sharps by pushing in the lever and coming back down. Boring yes, but that's what it takes to be able to get around in the different keys.

Take one key at a time and practice running up and down the scale until it gets fairly automatic, so that you don't have to think about each and every note. Spend at least fifteen to thirty minutes a day on this, more if you can cut it, then move on to another key, get used to it, and so on. C is an easy one to start with, no sharps or flats, all played with slide out. Follow the C scale with G, one sharp there, and so on. Once more—the aim here is to make the process mechanical. It's a matter of training yourself to do the right thing without having to think about it on a conscious level. There's no way I know of accomplishing this other than repetition. Every musician worth a damn did it.

Once you've become generally at home with the various scales, try bending notes. This is a lot harder on chromatic harps, the reeds are longer, stiffer and harder to work with. In fact, you'll probably find that the tongue-blocking method works better on chromatics. Lip pursing usually results in the note flatting out and not sounding. Patience and perseverance is the key.

Here's an example of chromatic harp work, this one uses electric harp. The tune "Chimes" is from the J. Geils album, *Ladies Invited* (Atlantic SD 77286). The harp break comes near the very end, following the lyrics, before the guitar solo. It's played in the key of D, but you don't have to touch the slide at all.

Chimes

(end break) Chromatic in D (slide out thru-out)

Vocal:
. . .I hear the chimes—

Wahhhhh-Ahhhhhhhhhhhhhhhhh
6↓   5&6↓

Wee-Eee-Eee-Eee-Ah-Wah-Ah-Wahhhhh
9↓   9↑   7↓   6↓   6↑   5↓   3↓   1↓

Wahhhhh-Wooooooooooooooooooo
6↓   5&6↓

Wee-Eee-Eee-Eee-Eee-Ah-Wah-Ah-Wah-Ah-Ah-A-Ooooooooooooooooo
9↓   9↑   7↓   6↓   6↑   5↓   3↓   3↑   2↓   1↓   1↓   1↓2&3↓

Wooooooooooo   *Weeeeeee-Ah-Eeeeeeeee*
3↑   3,4&5↓ 4↓ 3&4↑

Wahhh-Ooooooooooooo-Ah-Wah-Ooooo
3↓   3↓   3↑ 2↓ 1↓

Wah—Hah—Ooo—Wah—Ah—Hah—Ah—Hah—Ah—Wah—A—Doo!
6&7↓6&7↑ 5&6↓ 3&4↓3&4↑2&3↓2&3↑2&3↓2↓ 3↓   4↓ 5↓

The wavy lines above the phonetics indicate a warble (moving the harp back and forth across the lips). The last line is an approximation, playable from this transcription, but not guaranteed 100% accurate for it happens very fast. If this sound appeals to you, check out albums by bluesman Little Walter. This is a cop from his style and he's a master in it. (See the discography.)

Another thing you might want to try with a chromatic is learning to read sheet music. Even if the tunes aren't rock, they're still music, and you won't ever get to the point where you know too much.

Billy Joel *photo by James Shive*

Play Along Song Examples

Here are some specific songs to work on, by playing along with the recordings, most of which should be readily available. Do it the same way you did the previous examples. Put the record on first and while you're listening, read through the transcription to get the feel for it. Try playing from the page without the record, again until you've gotten the feel and the timing together. Now, put the record on and try playing with it.

The purpose of these examples is to give you a feel for how harp fits in with band backup, and the various melodic and rhythmic possibilities. Imitating what someone else played note-for-note is a step, but only a step for it takes more than duplication to be a creative musician. A tape recorder can do a more accurate job of copying than you can, however, a tape recorder can't create anything new, you can, and you ought to.

So these tunes are just a beginning—a way to practice timing, phrasing, and tone coloring. Unless noted otherwise, all the harp that's heard on any particular tune is included. Where there are vocal verses without harp, the lyrics are condensed to save space. It should be pretty obvious when you listen to the recordings.

Have fun. . .

The Promised Land

C Harp Crossed/2nd position

Intro:

Wah-Ah-Wah
3&4↓4↓ 3&4↓

Ah-Ooo-Ah-Wah
4↓ 5↑ 4↓ 4↓

Ah-Woo-Ah-Ooo
4↓ 5↑ 3↲ 3↲

Wah-Wah-Ah-A-Ooo
3↲ 3↓ 3↲ 3↑2↓

Vocal:

On a rattlesnake speedway in the Utah desert. . .

Instrumental break: (follows sax break)

Ooooooo	*A-Wah-Ah-Wah*	*Ah-Wah-Wah-Ooo*	*Woo-Woo-Ah-Ah-Woo*
3&4↓	4↓5↑ 4↓ 4↓	4↓ 5↑ 3↓ 3↓	3↓ 3↓ 3↓ 3↑ 2&3↓
Ooooooooo	*Wah-Wah-Ah-Ooo*	*Wah-Wah-Ah-Woo*	*Woo-Woo-Ah-Hah-Woo*
3&4↓	4↓ 5↑ 4↓ 4↓	4↓ 5↑ 3↓3↓	3↓ 3↓ 3↓ 3↑ 2&3↓

Vocal:

There's a dark cloud rising from the desert. . .

Out Chorus:

Vocal:

. . .I believe in the promised land

Out Chorus:

Vocal:

. . .I believe in the promised land

Wooooo	*Ah-Wah-Ah-Woo*	*Wah-Wah-Ah-Ooo*	*Ah-Hah-Ah-Wah-Ooo*
3&4↓	4↓ 5↑ 4↓ 4↓	4↓ 5↑ 3↓3↓	3↓3↓ 3↓3↑ 2&3↓
Wooooo	*Ah-Ooo-A-Woo*	*Wah-Wah-Ah-Ooo*	*Wah-Ah-Hah-Ah-Woo*
3&4↓	4↓5↗ 4↓4↓	4↓ 5↑ 3↓3↓	3↓ 3↓ 3↓ 3↑ 2&3↓

repeats 'till fade out

The tune is from Springsteen's third Columbia album. Basically it's a fourteen-note riff, repeated again and again, with slight variations in tone and timing. The hardest part is the jump in the third section, from 5 blow to 3 draw and bend. You have to hit the note bent, not sound it, then bend it. It may take a little work, but it's worth it.

Just Like A Woman

E Harp in 1st position

Intro:

Wooo	*Ooooo-Ahh-Ah-Woo*	*Wahh*
4&5↑	6↓ 6↑ 5↓ 5↑	4&5↑
Ahh	*Wee-Eee-Ah-Ooo*	
7↑	7↓ 6↓ 6↓ 6↑	

Vocal:

Nobody feels any pain. . .

Out Harp Chorus:

Vocal:

. . .but you break just like a little girl

Wahh-Ahh-Woo   /   *Ooo-Wah-Ahh-Doo*
4&5↓ 4&5↓ 4&5↑   6↓ 6↑ 5↓ 5↑

Ahh-Weeee   *Ooo-Wah-Ah-Wahh*
4&5↑ 7↑   7↓ 6↓ 6↑5&6↑

Wa-Wa-Doo   *Ah-Wah-Doo-Ah-Wah*
5↓ 5↓ 6↑   5↓ 5↑ 5↓ 5↑ 6↑

Wee-Eee-Ahh-Eee   *Wah-Ahh-Wah   Dooo-Wah*
7↑ 7↓ 6↓ 6↑   5&6↑5&6↓5&6↑ 4&5↓ 4↓

Ooo-Wah   Wahh-Ahhhhh   Wah-Ooo   /
4⌣ 4↓   4↑   3↑   3&4↓ 4&5↑

Wah-Wah-Ah-Doo   Wee-Eee-Ah-Dee
5↑ 5↑ 4↓ 4↑   6↑ 6↓ 6↑6↓

Eeee-Ahh-Eee-Ah-Wahh   Wee-Ah-Hah-Eee
6↑ 5↑ 5↑ 4↓ 4↑   7↑ 6↓ 6↑ 5↑

Ooo-Eee—Ooo—Wah-Hah-Eee
6↑ 7↑ 6↑ 6↑ 5↑ 4↑

Wah-Hah   Wahh   Hah-Ah-A-A-Doo
4↑ 4&5↓ 4&5↑   4↓ 5↓ 5↑4↓4↑

"Just Like a Woman" is from Bob Dylan's album, *Blonde On Blonde* (Columbia C2S 841) and is also included on his *Greatest Hits* (Columbia KCS 9463).

Dylan plays both guitar and harp here and the harp is in a rack holder which fits around his neck. The slash lines (/) indicate the start of a verse on the I chord. Those three tones which are in front, kind of jump time a bit. *An-ti-ci-pa-tion. . . .*

Remember, you're playing first position harp here.

Little Red Rooster

G Harp—cross/2nd position

Vocal:

. . .Since my little red rooster's been gone

A-Wah-Ah-Oooo   Eee   (guitar)
2↓4↑ 3↓ 2↓   6↑

Wah-Ah-Ooo   Eee   (guitar)
4↑ 3↓ 2↓   6↑

A-Wah-A-Ah-Ooo   (gtr)
5↓ 5↑ 4↓ 3↓ 2↓

Wah-A-Ah-Ooo   (gtr)
4↓ 4↑ 3↓ 2↓

Wah-Ah-Ah-Ooo   (gtr)
4↓ 4↑ 3↓ 2↓

Wah-Ah-Ah-Ooo   (gtr)
4↓ 4↑ 3↓ 2↓

Wah-Ah-Ooo-Eee   (gtr)
4↓ 4↑ 3↓ 2↓

Ah-Wah-Ahh-Ah-Ooo   (gtr)
5↓ 5↑ 4↓ 3↓ 2↓

Wah-Ah-Woo   (gtr)
4↓ 3↓ 2↓

Wah-Ah-Ooo-Eee   (gtr)
4↓ 4↑ 3↓ 2↓

Wah-Ah-Woo   (gtr)
4↑ 3↓ 2↓

                                          fades out

This is the Rolling Stones version of a Howling Wolf tune, heard on *The Rolling Stones Now!* (London PS 420). The harp and guitar alternate in the old blues call and response pattern. Jagger is blowing harp here.

Candy Man

C Harp 2nd position/cross

Intro:

Ahh-Ahh-A-Ahh-Oooo   *Woo-Woo-Ooooo*
2↓ 2↓ 3↓4↑ 4↓   4↓ 4↓ 4↑

Oooo   *Ahh*   *Oooo* *Wah-Ah-Ah-Ooo*
6↑   5↓   4↓   4↑ 3↓ 2↓ 2↓

Ah-Wah-Ooo   *Wah-Ah-Ah-Ooo*
3↓ 4↑ 4↓   4↑ 3↓ 2↓ 2↓

                         Ah-A-Ahh
                         1↓ 1↓1↓

Vocal:

Come on baby

        Wok   *Ah-Wah—Ooooo*
        2&3↓   2&3↓ 3&4↑ 3/4↓

Let me take you by the hand

Ah—A—Wah—Ah—Woooo̰o̰
2&3↓2&3↑2&3↓4↑   3/4↓

Ah-Hah-Ah-Oooo
4↑ 3↓ 2↓ 2↓

Come on sugar

Dah   Ooo-A-Wah-Ooo
2↓   3↓ 2↓ 4↑ 3↑

Let me take you by the hand

Wah—Ahh—Ooo—Wah
2&3↓ 2&3↑ 2&3↓ 2&3↑

Ooooo   Wah-Hah-Ah-Ooo
3&4↓   4↑ 3↓ 2↓ 2↓

You're for me

Oooo-Wah—Oooo
4↓   4 ⌣ 4↓

Let me be   Oooo-Wah-Ooo
4↓   4 ⌣ 4↓

Aw—your own candy—Your candy—Candy Man

Wah—Hah—Ah—O̰o̰oo̰o   Wah-Hah-Ah-Oooo
2&3↓ 2&3↑ 2&3↓3&4↓   4↑ 3↓ 2↓ 2↓

Ah-A-Ah
1↓ 1↓ 1↓

Vocal:

Come on baby. . .

Vocal:

. . .Candy Man

Break:

Ah-Wah-O̰o̰o̰o̰o̰o̰o̰o̰o̰oo   (guitar)
3↓ 4↑ 3&4/4&5↓

Wah-Hah-Ah-O̰o̰o̰oooooo   (guitar)
4↑ 3↓ 2↓ 2/3↓

Ah-Ooo-Wah-O̰o̰o̰oooooo   (guitar)
4↓ 4↑ 3↓ 3/2↑

Ah-Hah-Ah-Eeee   Wah-Ah-Eee
2↓ 3↓ 4↑ 6↑   5↓ 5↑ 4↓

Ah-A-Weeeeeeeee
4↓ 5↓ 6↓

Ooo-Wah-Oooo
6↑ 5↑ 6↑

Ahh-Wahh
5↓ 4↓

Ah-Hah-Ah-Ooo
4↑ 3↓ 2↓ 2↓

Ooo—Wah—Ooo
2&3↓ 3&4↑ 3&4↓

Wah-Hah-Ah-Ooo
4↑ 3↓ 2↓ 2↓

Ah-A-Ah
1↓ 1↓ 1↓

Vocal:

Come on woman. . .

Out Chorus

Vocal:

. . .Candy Man

Ah-Wah-Oooooo
3↓ 4↑ 3/4↓
Yeah candy

candy   candy

Ah-Hah-Ah-Wah
4↑ 3↓ 2↓ 2↓

Ah—Wah—Hah—Ahh
2&3↓ 2&3↓ 2&3↑ 2&3↓

I got a real tooth for you

Ah—Wah-Ooooooo
2&3↓ 4↑ 3&4↓

Wah-Hah-Ah-Oooo
4↑ 3↓ 2↓ 2↓

fades out

"Candy Man" was one of Roy Orbison's first big hit singles. Featured on harp at that time was the young session player Charlie McCoy. A few years later you heard his bass chord harp on Simon & Garfunkel's, "The Boxer." This version of "Candy Man" turns up on *The All Time Great Hits of Roy Orbison* (Monument MP 8600).

The brackets in the first and following verses indicate that the harp sometimes overlaps the vocal. Anything included within brackets is in the same time space. In other words, the first harp sound *Wok* happens at the same time the word "baby" is sung, and so on. Listen to the record, it's pretty clear.

Pills

A Harp 2nd/cross position

Intro:

Da-Dow-Oww
2↓ 2↓ 2↩

Ah-Wah-Ah-Ah-Ah-Ooo
3↓ 3 ↑ 2↑ 3↓ 2↓ 3↓

De-Dowwwww   *Da-Doo*   *Ooooooooooo*
2↓ 2↓   2↓ 2↓   3/4↓

Wah-Ah-Oo-Ah-Ah-Ah   *Ah-Wah-Ooo-Ah*
4↓ 4↑ 3↓ 2↓ 3↓ 3↓   2↓ 3↓ 2↓ 2↵

Ooo-Wah   *Ooo-Ahh*   *Ooo-Wah*   *Ooo-Woo*   *Ooo*
4↵ 4↓   4↵ 4↓   4↵ 4↓   4↵ 4↓   4↓

Vocal:

As I was lying in a hospital bed. . .

Out Chorus Break:

Vocal:

. . .as I was lying in a hospital bed—I said—

Da-Da-Dut-Dow-Ow   *Ooo-Wah-Ah-Oww*
2↓ 2↓ 2↓ 2↓   2↵   4↓ 3↓ 2↓ 3↓

Woo-Ah   *Woo-Ah*   *Wooooooooooooo*
3↓ 2↓   3↓ 2↓   3/4↓

Wah-Hah-Ooo-Hah-Ah-Oww   *Ah-Hah-Ah-Ooo*
4↓ 4↑ 3↓ 2↓ 3↓ 3↓   3↓ 3↑ 2↑ 2↓

Ahh   *Wahh*   *Ooo*   *Wahh*   *Ahh-Wah-Ah-*
4↓   4↑   3↓   2↑   3↓ 3↑ 2↑

A-Oooooooooooooooooooo—Woo !
2↓2↵   2↓

The New York Dolls were really the first of the New Wave or Punk groups, but they were a bit ahead of their time, and had splintered into several directions by the time the music scene was ready for them. Lead vocalist, songwriter, and mouth harp player, David JoHansen had a solo career going, while other members were in and out of various bands.

"Pills" is a Bo Diddley tune from their first album *New York Dolls* (Mercury SRML-675). In the second line of each section, the wavy line over the *Ooooo* or *Woooo* means that it's played with a hand warble. To do this the harp moves back and forth rapidly as you alternate between holes 3 and 4.

Section 43

G Harp 2nd position/cross
Follows guitar and organ introduction

1st Chorus:

(A-Wa-A-Da-)   *Eeeeeeeeeeeeeeeeeeeeeee*
4↓ 5↓ 6↓ 8↓   9↓

Ahh-Eeeeee   *Ah-Wah-Ooooooooooooo*
8↓ 8↑   7↑ 8↑ 8↓

Ahh-Ooooooo   Ahh-Oooo-Wah-Ah-Wahhhhhhhh
7↓ 7↑   6↑ 6↵ 6↓ 6↵6↓

Ah-Wah-Hah-Ah-Ooo   Ah-Dah-Ooo-Woooooooooo
6↑6↓ 6↑ 5↑ 5↓   5↑ 4↓ 4↵ 4↓

2nd Chorus:

(Wah-Ah-Hah)-   Eeeeeeeeeeeeeeeeeeeeeeeeeeee
4↓ 5↓ 6↓   9↓

Ah-Hah-Ah-Eee   Ah—Ooo-Wahhhhhhhhhhhhhh
9↑ 9↓ 8↓ 8↑   7↑ 8↑ 8↓

Ahh-Ooo-Ahh-   Wooooooo-Oooooooooooooo
7↓ 7↑ 6↑   6↵   6↓

Ah-Wah-Ah-Hah-Ooo   Ah-Woo   Woo-Wahhhhhhhhh
6↑6↓ 6↑ 5↑ 5↓   5↓ 4↓ 4↵ 4↓

3rd Chorus:

Ahh-Ah-Wah-Ahh-Ooooo   Oooo Woo-Ahh-Oooo-Wah
4↑ 4↓ 5↓ 5↑ 5↓   6↑   5↓ 5↑ 4↓ 4↑

Hah-Ah-Ahh-Ooooo   Ooo Woo-Hah-Ah-Ooo-Wah-Hah
4↓ 5↓ 5↑ 5↓   6↑ 6↓ 6↑ 5↓5↑ 4↓ 4↑

                        -Ah-Wah-Ah-Hah-Ah-Wah-Hah-Ah
                        4↓ 5↓ 5↑ 5↓ 6↑ 6↓ 6↑ 5↓

                        -Wah-Oooooooooooooo-Wooooooo
                        4↓ 4↵   4↓

4th Chorus:

Weee-Ahh-Eeee   Eee-Hee-A-Ahh-Eee
8↓ 8↑ 9↓   9↑ 9↓ 8↓8↑ 8↓

Eeee   Wee-Hee-Ah-Eee Eee-Hee-A-Ahh-Eee
7↑   8↓ 8↓ 8↑ 9   9↑ 9↓ 8↓8↑ 8↓

Ahh-Weeee Ah-Weeeee Ah-Wahh-Hah-Ahh-Ahh
7↑ 7&8↓ 7↑ 7&8↓   7↑7↓ 6↓ 5↓ 5↑

                      Wah Ooo-Wooooooooo
                      4↓ 4↵ 3&4↓

5th Chorus:

Ahhh-Weeeeeeeeeeeeeeeeeeeeee Ah-Wah-Ah-A-Eeeeeeee
4↓ 9↓   8↓8↑ 7↑8↑8↓

Ahh-Wahh-Ahh Ooo-Wooooo Ah-Woo-A-Ah-Ah
7↓ 7↑ 6↑   6↵ 6↓   6↑ 7↓ 6↓5↓ 5↑

                          Ooo-Woooooooooooooooooooooo
                          4↵ 3&4/4&5↓

This song is an instrumental from the first album by Country Joe and the Fish—*Electric Music For the Mind and Body* (Vanguard VRS 79244). One of the better of the West Coast acid-rock groups, the Fish went on to fame at Woodstock, and eventually split up. Joe McDonald, who plays harp here, has gone on to a solo recording career.

The phrases in brackets at the beginning of both the first and second chorus are really fast, it's just a run up the harp. There are some nice little unexpected variations on a basic theme going on here, check it out.

Everybody's Crying Mercy

G Harp 1st position

Intro:

Uh   Un-Wuhh   Wuhh   Wuhh   Wuhh   Wuhh   Wuh   Wuh
4↑   4↑ 4↑   4↑   4↑   4↑   4↑   4↑   4↑

Wah—Ahh—Ah-Ooooooo-Ooooooooo-Wahhhhh-Ooo-Ahhhhh
3↓   3↑   2↑ 1↑   2↑   3↑   3↓ 3↓

Vocal:

I don't believe the things I'm seeing   Wah-Ahh-Ah-Oooo
                                          3↓ 3↑ 2↑ 1↑

I been wondering about some things I heard
Everybody's cryin' mercy   Ah-Wah-Oooo-Ah
                                   2↓ 2↓ 2↑   1↑

When they don't know the meaning of the word

A bad enough situation   Ah   Wah-Ah-Ah-Ooo
                           3↓   3↓ 3↑ 2↑ 1↑

Is sure enough getting worse
Everybody's cryin' justice—
Just as soon as there's business first
Toe-to-toe touch and go .
Give a cheer and get your souvenir
Well you know the people running round in circles   Ah-Wooo-Ah
                                                      3↑ 2↑   1↑

Don't know what they're headed for   Ah-Wah-Ooo
                                        3↓ 4↑ 3↑

Everybody's cryin' peace on earth
Just as soon as we win this war

Harp break:

Wah-Wah *Oooooooooooooooo-Wah-Oo-A-Wah-Ahhhh-Ooooooo*
4↑ 4↑ 3↑ 3↑ 3↑ 2↑1↑ 2↑ 4↑

Uhh-Uhh *Uhh-Unnh* *Unnh-Ooo*
4↑ 4↑ 4↑ 4↑ 4↑ 3↓

Ahh—A—Woo—Oo—A—Woo—Ah—Wah
2↓ 3↓ 2↓ 2↓ 2↓ 2↓ 1↑ 2↑

Ah-Wah—Ah-Ah-Oo-Ah-A-Wah *Wah-Oooooo*
3↑ 3↑ 3↑ 2↑ 4↑ 4↑ 3↑2↑ 2↑ 1↑

Straight ahead, gotta knock 'em dead
So pack your kit, choose your own hypocrite
Don't have to go to off Broadway *Wah-Ah-Ooo*
3↑ 2↑ 1↑

To see something plain absurb
Everybody's crying mercy
when they don't know the meaning of the word
No—they don't know the meaning of the word

This Mose Allison tune is a bluesy ballad with a nice sardonic swing to it. It's sung here by Bonnie Raitt, on her album, *Taking My Time* (Warner BS 2729) and features Taj Mahal on harp. Taj is of course well known in his own right and has recorded several albums featuring blues and soulful music on Columbia. His accompaniment here is much in the style of Chicago bluesman Sonny Boy Williamson. It's simple, sparse, and effective. Also, it's in first position harp.

Low Rider

C Harp cross/2nd position

Vocal:

All my friends know the Low Rider
The Low Rider is a little higher

Riff:

Dut-Dut-Dut-Dut-Dut *Da-Dut*
3↓ 3↓ 3↓ 3↓ 3↓ 4↑ 4↓

Dut *Da-Dah* *Dee-Dah*
2↓ 3↓ 4↑ 3↓ 2↓

Dut-Dut-Dut-Dut-Dut *Da-Dut*
3↓ 3↓ 3↓ 3↓ 3↓ 4↑ 4↓

Dut *Da-Dah* *Dee-Dah*
2↓ 3↓ 4↑ 3↓ 2↓

Dut-Dut-Dut-Dut-Dut

2♪ 2♪ 2♪ 2♪ 2♪

Dut-Dut-Dut-Dut-Dut

2♪ 2♪ 2♪ 2♪ 2♪

Dah-Ooooooooooooooooooooo

2♪ 2↓

Vocal:

Low Rider drives a little slower
Low Rider is a real goer

Riff (as above)

Vocal:

Low Rider knows every street, yeah
Low Rider is the one to meet, yeah

Riff (as above)

Vocal:

Low Rider don't use no gas now
Low Rider don't drive too fast

Riff (as above)

Vocal:

Take a little trip, take a little trip
take a little trip and see
Take a little trip, take a little trip
take a little trip with me

Riff (as above)   fades out

"Low Rider" features the harp playing of Lee Oskar, who has since gone solo, but for several years played with War. This song appears on *War—Greatest Hits* (United Artists LA 648).

It's a good example of the use of a simple, little riff repeated over and over. In fact, there are no more than six different notes used here, but it's really a fitting little sound. Proof that sometimes the simplest is best.

Pretty Thing

A Harp 2nd position/crossed

Vocal:	Harp:
You pretty thing	*Ooo-Wah—Ooo* 3&4↓ 4↑ 3↓
Let me buy you wedding ring	*Ah-Ah-Ooo-Wah-Ooo-Wah-Ahh* 4↓ 5↑ 5↓ 5↑ 4↓ 4↑ 3↓
Let me hear the choir sing	*Ah-Ah-Ooo-Wah-Ooo-Wah-Ahh* 4↓ 5↑ 5↓ 5↑ 4↓ 4↑ 3↓
Oh—You pretty thing	*Oooooo Wah Ooo* 3&4↓ 1↓ 2↓
You pretty thing	*Oooo-Wah-Ooo* 3&4↓ 4↑ 3↓
Let me walk you down the aisle	*Ah-Ah-Ooo-Wah-Ooo-Wah-Ahh* 4↓ 5↑ 5↓ 5↑ 4↓ 4↑ 3↓
Smile & wear a lover's smile	*Ah-Ah-Ooo-Wah-Ooo-Wah-Ahh* 4↓ 5↑ 5↓ 5↑ 4↓ 4↑ 3↓
Oh—You pretty thing	*Oooooo Wah Ooo* 3&4↓ 1↓ 2↓

(guitar break)

Wahhhhhhhhhhhhhhh   *Ooooooooooooooooooo*
2&3/3&4↓   5↓

Ah-Woo-Ah-Wahh   *Wah-Ah*
5↑ 4↓ 4↑ 3↓   3↓ 2↓

Ah-Wahh(-Wah-Ah-A)   *Wahh-Wahh-Ah-Ooo*   *Ah-Wah(-Ah-A-A)*
2↓ 2↓ 2↓ 2↓1↓   3↓ 3↓ 3↓ 2↓   2↓ 2↓ 2↓ 2↓1↓

Let me kiss you gentle	*Ooo-Wah-Ooo* 3&4↓ 4↑ 3↓
Squeeze & hug you tight	*Ah-Ah-Ooo-Wah-Ooo-Wahh-Ahh* 4↓ 5↑ 5↓ 5↑ 4↓ 4↑ 3↓
Let me give you all my love	*Ah-Ah-Ooo-Wah-Ooo-Wah-Ahh* 4↓ 5↑ 5↓ 5↑ 4↓ 4↑ 3↓
The rest of my life	*Oooooo Wah Ooo* 3&4↓ 4↓ 2↓
You pretty thing	*Ooo-Wah-Ooo* 3&4↓ 4↑ 3↓
Let me hold you by my side	*Ah-Ah-Ooo-Wah-Ooo-Wah-Ahh* 4↓ 5↑ 5↓ 5↑ 4↓ 4↑ 3↓

Stand before my blushing bride.	*Ah-Ah-Ooo-Wah-Ooo-Wah-Ahh* 4↓ 5↑ 5↓ 5↑ 4↓ 4↑ 3↓
You pretty thing	*Ooooooo Wah Ooo* 3&4↓ 1↓ 2↓
You pretty thing	*Ooo-Wah-Ooo* 3&4↓4↑ 3↓
Let me dedicate my life	*Ah-Ah-Ooo-Wah-Ooo-Wah-Ahh* 4↓ 5↑ 5↓ 5↑ 4↓ 4↑ 3↓
You will always be my wife	*Ah-Ah-Ooo-Wah-Ooo-Wah-Ahh* 4↓ 5↑ 5↓ 5↑ 4↓ 4↑ 3↓
Oh—You pretty thing	*Oooooo Wah Ooo* 3&4↓ 1↓ 2↓
	Wahh Wahh Wahh etc. 2↓ 2↓ 2↓
(guitar)	
	fades out

Bo Diddley is of course one of the first of the rock and roll guitar players. His own distinctive sound has been carried on for some time. This track can be found on his *Greatest Hits* (Checker 2989) and it features Billy Boy Arnold, a Chicago blues harp player who had several singles of his own out in the 50s. Arnold plays an electric harp here, through an amplifier, which accounts for its echo sound. The wavy line over the first tone in the break indicates a warble again, alternating between holes 2 and 3 and holes 3 and 4. The phrases in brackets happen *real* fast.

Georgia Swing

D Harp cross/2nd position

Vocal:

. . .ain't gonna worry 'bout a doggone thing

Ah-Wah-Ooooooooooooooooooooooooooo 3↓ 4↑ 3-4-5↓	*Ooo-Wah* 4↓ 2↓
Aww-(Oo)-Wooooooooooooooooooooooo 3↓ 4↵ 3-4-5↓	*Ooo-Wah-Wah* 4↓ 2↓ 2↓

Doo-Wah 2↑ 2↓	*Ahh-Ahh-Ah-Ooo* 3↓ 3↓ 3↵3↑	*Wah-Ahh* 2↑ 3↑
Ahh-Ahh-Ah 3↓ 3↓ 3↵	*Ooo-Wah-Ah* 3↑ 2↑ 3↑	*Ahh-Ooo-Ah-Ooo* 3↓ 4↓ 5↑ 4↓
Woo-Ah 5↑ 4↓	*Ooo-Wah-Ah-Ooo* 3&4↓3&4↓4↑ 3↓	
Ah-Wah 3↓ 4↑	*Ooo-Ah—Ooo-Ah-Aw-Wah-Ah* 4↵ 4↓ 4↵ 4↓ 4↓ 3↓ 2↓	

Ah-Wah-Ah-Ah-Ooo-Ooo-Wah-Wah-Ooooo
3↓ 3↓ 3↓3↓ 3↑ 3↑ 2↑ 2↑ 2↓

Ah-Wah-Ah-A-Ooo   Ah-Wah
3↓ 4↑ 3↓ 3↓2↓   2↓ 1↓

Ah-Wah-Ah-   Ooooooooooooooooooo   Ooo-Wah-Ah
2↓3↓   4↓   3-4-5↓   4↓ 3↓ 2↓

Ah-Wooooooooooooooooooooooo   Ah-Wah-Wah-Da-Da-Ah
3↓ 3-4-5↓   3↓ 2↓ 2↓ 2↓2↓2↓

Ah-Ah-Ah-Ooo-Ooo-Ah-Ah   Ah-Ah-Ah   Ooo-Wah-Ah
3↓ 3↓ 3↓3↑ 3↑ 2↑ 3↑   3↓ 3↓3↓   3↑ 2↓ 1↓

Ooo-Wah-Hah-Ahh-Ooo   Wah-Hah   Woo-Ah-Hah-Ooo
3↓   3↓ 3&4↑3&4↓2&3↑ 2&3↓2&3↑ 4&5↓3&4↑3&4↓2&3↓

Wahh-Ahh-Eeeeeeeee   Ah-Hah-Oooo   Wah-Ahh
3↓   4↑ 4↓   4↓ 4↓ 2↓   2↓ 1↓

Ah-Eeee-Eeee-Ah-Wah-Ah   Ah-Ah-Oooo
4↓ 5↓ 5↓ 5↑4↑ 3↑   3↓ 3↓2↓

Ah-Wah-Ooo-Ooo   Ah-Wah-Ooo
3↓ 4↑ 3↓ 3↓   2↓1↓ 1↓

James Cotton was with Muddy Waters for a number of years. He went out on his own, and eventually cut several albums, ranging in styles from pure blues and soul, to a hybrid of blues and rock styles. The track from "Georgia Swing" illustrates this. The album *Taking Care of Business* recorded by The James Cotton Blues Band (Capitol ST-814), was produced by Todd Rundgren. It features some guitar work by Johnny Winter and Mike Bloomfield, and a tune by Bob Dylan. Although it doesn't always work, the album is an interesting experiment in cross-breeding.

The harp here is amplified, and sometimes drowned out by a chanting chorus, so accuracy is not 100% guaranteed, but it's close enough to play.

I Should Have Known Better

C Harp cross/2nd position

Intro:

Ah—A—Wah   Hah—Ahh—Hah   Ab—A—Wah   Hah—Ahh—Hah.
3&4↓3↓3&4↓ 3&4↑ 3&4↓ 3&4↑   3&4↓3↓3&4↓   3&4↑3&4↓ 3&4↑

Ah—A—Wah   Hah—Ahh—Hah   Ab   Wah—Hah-Ah—Ah
3&4↓3↓3&4↓ 3&4↑ 3&4↓3&4↑   3&4↓ 3&4↑3&4↓3&4↑3&4↓

Vocals:

I should have known better with a girl like you. . .

Vocal:

. . .and I do

Ah—A—Wah   Hah—Ah—Ah
3&4↓3↓ 3&4↓ 3&4↑3&4↓3&4↑

Ooo-Wah   Wah—Hah—Ah—Ah
3&4↓3&4↓ 3&4↑3&4↓3&4↑3&4↓

Vocal:

Woe—Oh—I never realized what a kiss could be. . .

Vocal:

. . .say you love me too

                  Ah—Wah—Hah—Ah—Hah
                 3&4↓3&4↓3&4↑3&4↓3&4↑

Ah—A—Wah   Hah—Ahh-Wah—Ah
3&4↓3↓3&4↓ 3&4↑3&4↓3&4↑3&4↓

Vocal:

So—Woe—I shoulda realized. . .

Vocal:

. . .give me more

      Ooo—Ah—Wah   Hah—Ah—Hah   Ooo-Ah-Wah   Hah—Ah—Hah
      3&4↓3↓ 3&4↓ 3&4↑3&4↓3&4↑ 3&4↓3↓3&4↓ 3&4↓3&4↑3&4↓

Guitar break:

Ooo—Wah—Hah-Ah—Ah   *Ooo—Wah—Hah—Hah-Ooo*
3&4↓3&4↓3&4↑3&4↓3&4↑   *3&4↓3&4↓3&4↑3&4↓3&4↑*

Ooo—Wah—Hah-Hah—Ah   *Ooo—Wah—Hah—Hah-Ooo*
3&4↓3&4↓3&4↑3&4↓3&4↑   *3&4↓3&4↓3&4↑3&4↓3&4↑*

Ooo—Wah—Hah—Ahh-Ooo   *Oooooooooooooooooooo*
3&4↓3&4↓3&4↑3&4↓3&4↑   *2&3↓*

Wahhhhhhhhhhhhhhhh   *Ahhhhhhhhhhhhhhhh*
2&3↑   *4&5↓*

Wah—Wah—Hah—Ah—Wah   *Ah—A—Wah-Hah-Ah—Wah—Ah*
3&4↓3&4↓3&4↑ 3&4↓3&4↑   *3&4↓3↓3&4↓3&4↑3&4↓3&4↑3&4↓*

Vocal:

Woe—oh I never realized. . .

Vocal:

. . .say you loved me too

Ah-Wah   Hah—Ahh—Ah
3&4↓3&4↓3&4↑ 3&4↓ 3&4↑

Ooo—A—Wah—Hah—Ah—Ah
3&4↓ 3↓3&4↓ 3&4↑ 3&4↓3&4↑

Vocal:

you loved me too

Ooo—A—Wah—Hah—Ah—Ah
3&4↓ 3↓3&4↓ 3&4↑ 3&4↓3&4↑

Ooo-A—Wah—Hah—Ah—Ah
3&4↓3↓ 3&4↓ 3&4↑ 3&4↓ 3&4↑

Vocal:

you loved me too

Ooo—Wah   Hah—Ah—Ah   Ooo—Wah—Hah—Ah—Hah
3&4↓3&4↓ 3&4↑3&4↓3&4↑   3&4↓ 3&4↓ 3&4↑ 3&4↓ 3&4↑

Vocal:

you loved me too   fades out

"I Should Have Known Better" turns up on the Beatles *Hey Jude* collection (Capitol SW 385).

John Lennon overdubbed the harp here. Like many of the early English R&R mixes, the harp is isolated on one side channel rather than mixed in the middle, so it's easier to hear. This is a nice mix of chords and occasional bent single tones.

The lyrics have been condensed but the parts where harp is heard are included in full.

Creative Playing

What you've been doing here so far is learning how to play like other people, copying riffs from existing tunes. The next step is to make your own music. This involves taking your basic chops and vocabulary of styles and saying something with your own voice. Copying is almost essential to learning, but you have to go beyond this to call yourself a musician.

You must have ideas of your own about the music you want to play so now's the time to start getting into it. Play with ideas and if you get a little melody line running through your head, mess with it. Try it fast, try it slow, try it inside-out. Change accents, vary the rhythm, and play with all the various possibilities. Don't worry too much about blowing something that's never been played before for odds are that it has, somewhere. Maybe you can play it better than it's ever been done before and that's worth the effort. Keep your mind open and you'll find most likely, that ideas come to you at really weird times. If you're too busy with something else to explore it right then, save it, let it cook awhile, and work on it when you've got the space to do it.

A good riff can be just as important as a melody line—riffs are what make tunes work. A song with a catchy and repeated "hook" stays in your head as long as a whole six chorus exposition even if it's only four bars long.

However, don't be afraid to try for whole pieces. If you hear something that needs several choruses, go with it and try it out with other people to see how, why, and if it works. But don't give up if it don't fall into place just like that. Give it at least several chances. Nothing may happen the first, second, or even third time. The next time it may catch fire.

Music, and the way it's received, depends on a lot of variables. A good tune can fall flat just 'cause an audience may be too hot, too cold, too drunk, or too sober. You have to try it under different circumstances before you know for sure how it'll work. Tunes that sounded dynamite down in the basement may just fade away in a gig. Tunes that you thought were throwaway numbers may get a whole club up and screaming. That's part of the whole magic and mysterious chemistry of music, a matter of being in the right place at the right time with the right riff.

Harp ain't always a lead instrument and a lot of times your job will be to add accents and fill in holes. What really counts is how well the whole band comes off and not just how flashy you are. Real music doesn't always have a lot to do with ego-strokes and if all you care about is how *you* sound then you should probably be out disco dancing instead. If you're into playing music right you'll be aware that there are times when you should shut up altogether and there are times when three right notes are just as effective as fifteen fast and flashy ones.

Band music is the integration of a lot of parts, sounds and colors so making sure that the mix is right oughta be the most important goal. There will be times for you to soar on a solo and blow your soul, but it oughta be in the right place. *Learn to listen* for there will be times when you should be just comping on rhythm 'cause somebody else is hot on a solo, when it's your turn they'll do the same for you.

Once you've got your chops down and know how to blow your way around, let your mind follow its footsteps and try new paths. Be ready for ideas which may crawl out of the woodwork and try to temper them so that they become a source of inspiration.

Music is a part of us that cannot be put into words. Learn to let it sing through you. On nights when you least expect it you may find that you'll be playing something which may magically reach you, your band, and your audience.

With any luck it'll happen just often enough to keep you pushing on and that's most of the battle of staying alive—keepin' on keepin' on. The rest of it is to be able to share and maybe touch someone with it. If nothing else, maybe you can get people to dance—that helps too. . . .

Okay, that's about all I can say. The rest is up to you.

Come on—surprise me. . . .

The Notation Decoded

All of the following is explained as it comes up in the text. It's included here in a chunk in case you have the kind of mind that likes to see things in a neat pile.

Melody Exercises

5 4 4 4 5 5 5
↑ ↓ ↑ ↓ ↑ ↑ ↑

The number indicates the hole to play, the direction of the arrow indicates a blow or draw note (pointing up means blow, pointing down means draw), length of the arrow shows the relative length of time to hold each tone.

Phonetics

Wah-Doo-Ahh
3↑   2↓ 3↑

Each harp tone is represented by a word similar to the sound of the tone. Again, the number indicates which hole to play, the arrow shows whether to blow or draw.

Wah-Doo
3↓   2↓

This indicates that the two separate tones are played, they are slurred together instead of being articulated.

Time-Rhythm Exercises

Dit-Dit   Dah   Hah-A-Hah
3↓ 3↓   2↓   3↓ 3↑ 3↓

Each line above the phonetics is a time unit. The length of the line doesn't matter. In the example above, the basic unit is the *Dah* sound and it's one unit, foot-tap, whatever. The first two notes *Dit-Dit* take the same time to play together as the one *Dah* note. The *Hah-A-Hah* phrase indicates three notes should be played in the same time it would take to play one *Dah* note.

Dit DAH-Dit Oooooo
2↓ 3↓   2↓ 2↑

In this example the phonetic which is capitalized *DAH* should be played a bit harder than the other notes. The basic time unit here is the first note, *Dit*. The *DAH-Dit* notes are each half as long as that *Dit*. The two lines over the *Oooooo* indicate that it should be held twice as long as the *Dit* (if there were three lines, you would hold it three times, etc.)

Bent Notes

Wah-Ooo   Eee-Ahh
2↓ 2↓   7↑ 7↑

This example illustrates bending notes. On the first phrase you draw in on hole 2 and play *Wah*, then you bend that note down in pitch and play *Ooo*. The bent arrow is a bent tone. In the second half of the example, you blow hole 7, and play *Eee* then bend it down in pitch, to play *Ahh*. An arrow pointing down is a draw note, an arrow pointing up is a blow note as before, but in both cases the bend is always lower in pitch.

Woooooooooooooo
  3&4↓ / 2&3↓

In this example of the hand warble the harp is moved rapidly back and forth across the lips while you draw in holes 3 and 4 and alternate with 2 and 3. They are *not* separate tones, they are blended together in the warble.

Discography

This list includes all the source examples from the text, in the order in which they appear.

The Beatles	*The Early Beatles*	Capitol ST 2309
	Meet The Beatles	Capitol ST 2047
Rolling Stones	*Rolling Stones*	London LL 3375
Jimmy Reed	*Very Best of Jimmy Reed*	Buddah BDS 4003
	History of Jimmy Reed	Trip TLP 8012
Little Walter	*Little Walter*	Chess 2 ACMB-202
Willie Nelson	*Red Headed Stranger*	Columbia KC 33482
Rolling Stones	*Let it Bleed*	London NPS-4
J. Geils Band	*Ladies Invited*	Atlantic SD 77286
Bruce Springsteen	*Darkness on the Edge of Town*	Columbia JC 35318
Bob Dylan	*Blonde on Blonde*	Columbia C2S 841
	Greatest Hits	Columbia KCS 9463
Rolling Stones	*The Rolling Stones Now!*	London PS 420
Roy Orbison	*All Time Greatest Hits*	Monument MP 8600
New York Dolls	*New York Dolls*	Mercury SRML-675
Country Joe & the Fish	*Electric Music for the Mind and Body*	Vanguard VRS 79244
Bonnie Raitt	*Taking My Time*	Warner BS 2729
War	*Greatest Hits*	United Artists LA 648
Bo Diddley	*Greatest Hits*	Checker 2989
James Cotton	*Taking Care of Business*	Capitol ST 814
Canned Heat	*Very Best of Canned Heat*	United Artists LA-431
The Beatles	*Hey Jude*	Capitol SW 385

These albums are not cited in the text, but may be of interest to special harp fans.

Blues

Sonny Boy Williamson	*Sonny Boy Williamson*	Chess 2ACMB-206
	King Biscuit Time	Arhoolie 2020
Sonny Terry	*Midnight Special*	Fantasy F-24721

Country

Willie Nelson	*Willie & Family * Live*	Columbia 35642
Charlie McCoy	*The World of Charlie McCoy*	Monument 18097

Rock

Stevie Wonder	*Fulfillingness First Finale*	Tamala T6 33251

John Lennon *photo by David Gahr*